AP® U.S. History
EXPRESS

AP® U.S. History
EXPRESS

KAPLAN)

PUBLISHING

New York

© 2010 by Kaplan, Inc.

Published by Kaplan Publishing, a division of Kaplan, Inc.
395 Hudson Street
New York, NY 10014

Printed in the United States of America

10 9 8 7 6 5 4 3 2 1

ISBN 978-1-60714-786-2

Kaplan Publishing books are available at special quantity discounts to use for sales promotions, employee premiums, or educational purposes. For more information or to purchase books, please call the Simon & Schuster special sales department at 866-506-1949.

Table of Contents

How to Take the Test

◆◆ ABOUT THIS BOOK

If you are taking an AP U.S. History course at your high school, or if you have a good foundation in historical analysis and strong composition skills, taking the exam can help you earn college credit and placement into advanced coursework. Think of the money and time you can save! It can also improve your chances of acceptance to competitive schools, because colleges know that AP students are better prepared for college.

In the following pages, you will find information about the format of the exam, test-taking strategies, and an extensive review of essential topics that will help you to identify your strengths and weaknesses, and establish a study plan.

The first thing you need to do is find out what is on the AP U.S. History exam. The next section of this introduction presents the overall test structure and a brief overview of its scoring. You'll find background information about the test and the most effective test strategies to help you score your best, including guidelines for successful multiple-choice testing and essay construction.

◆◆ ABOUT THE TEST

The AP U.S. History exam is 3 hours and 5 minutes long. You will have 55 minutes to complete the first section, which consists of 80 multiple choice questions. You will have 2 hours and 10 minutes to complete the second section, which consists of 3 essay questions.

Section I: Multiple-choice	80 questions	55 minutes	50% of the exam
Section II: Essays	3 questions	130 minutes	50% of the exam

The exam covers the period from the first European explorations of the Americas to the present. However, there is a gap between when the test is created and when it is administered. You do *not* need to know current events or the very recent past. The majority of questions are about the nineteenth and twentieth centuries.

Time Period and Weight on the Exam

Pre-Columbian to 1789	20%
1790 to 1914	45%
1915 to the present	35%

In addition to the major time periods, questions on the AP U.S. History exam reflect the following areas of historical inquiry:

I.   social change, and cultural and intellectual developments (40%)
II. political institutions, behavior, and public policy (35%)
III. diplomacy and international relations (15%)
IV. economic developments (10%)

Use these topics as a guideline to help you focus your study.

For more information about the AP U.S. History exam and other AP exams, check the College Board AP website at **apcentral.collegeboard.com.**

❯❯ WHAT THE TEST REQUIRES

Although the AP U.S. History exam is not a test that one passes or fails, generally a 3 or higher on the 5-point scale is necessary to receive advanced placement, credit, or both from the college of your choice.

The best way to find out what the test requires is to look at the practice sections in this book. They include detailed explanations for the answers to each question. There are sample student responses for each essay question and a commentary from an "AP reader" who will tell you why the response received the score it did. Use the scoring guides provided and these commentaries to get a sense of your own strengths and weaknesses.

The AP U.S. History exam tests your analytical skills and factual knowledge. The multiple-choice and essay questions require you to apply key historical events and issues. However, the exam does not test your knowledge of specific dates. You will also be asked to interpret historical data, establish connections, and draw meaningful conclusions.

❯❯ HOW THE EXAM IS SCORED

The multiple-choice section makes up half of your score. Your score for the multiple-choice section is based on the total number of correct answers. No points are deducted for wrong answers. The essay section makes up the other half of your score. Your essays are read and graded by trained AP teachers and college faculty. These two scores are combined to give a composite score, which is converted to the AP's 5-point scale.

All AP exams are rated on a scale of 1 to 5, with 5 as the highest:

5 Extremely well qualified
4 Well qualified
3 Qualified
2 Possibly qualified
1 No recommendation

> ❯ AP EXPERT TIP
>
> Many states post online or offer in hard copy the AP test score requirements for the various colleges and universities within the state. These will vary from state to state, just as score requirements vary from college to college.

◆❱ HOW TO APPROACH THE MULTIPLE-CHOICE SECTION

A large number of multiple-choice questions are about such topics as the impact of legislation on the economy and social groups, and the effects on political processes by social, economic, and cultural developments. Many questions pertain to more than one area of historical inquiry.

Here are some tips for doing well on the multiple-choice section of the test:

Answer in Your Own Order

Rather than taking the test in a completely linear way, use these steps:

1. Answer all the questions that you know and are sure about first.

2. Go through the questions you were not sure about and mark them based on your familiarity with the topic.
   - If the topic is familiar and you can eliminate at least two answer choices, mark the question by **circling** the question number, and move on.
   - If you do *not* remember the topic, mark the question with an **X**, and move on.

3. Go back through the test and answer the questions circled. Try to eliminate at least three choices, then take your best guess.

4. Go back and answer the questions you marked with an X. Again, try to eliminate at least two or three choices, and take an educated guess.

Read Actively

The main part of a test question, before the answer choices, is called the *stem*. Read the question stem carefully, paying particular attention to key words such as *only, except, always, not, never, best*. Underline key words and phrases in the question.

Predict an Answer

Before you look at the answer choices, try to think of the answer on your own. This will help you narrow the choices and avoid being seduced by wrong answers that *seem* right at first glance. Wrong answer choices are also known as *distracters* because they *distract* you from the right answer.

Use the Process of Elimination

As you read through the possible responses, cross off the ones you know are wrong. Be sure to read every possible answer before you make your selection. When eliminating distracters think about whether each choice is outside of the time period, region, or category of the question.

Pace Yourself

You have 55 minutes to complete 80 questions. Move quickly but thoroughly through the test. Do not linger on any single question for more than about 30 seconds.

If you have time remaining after you have completed all of the questions, go back and check your answers and check to make sure you have gridded in all responses correctly.

Remember, every correct answer adds to your score, and <u>there is no penalty for incorrect answers.</u> **So be sure to answer every question!**

Practice multiple-choice questions, with detailed answer explanations, are provided at the ends of chapters 1, 2, and 4.

❯❯ HOW TO APPROACH THE ESSAY QUESTIONS

The second part of the AP U.S. History exam is the essay section. This section inspires the most dread in the minds of students taking the test. However, understanding the structure, timing, and scoring of the essays can give you a big advantage.

Part A, the document-based question (DBQ), asks you to analyze information based on several historical documents provided. It typically requires you to relate the documents to a major historical period or theme. A sample DBQ question is provided at the end of Chapter 3.

Part B presents two standard free-response questions (FRQs). Choose and answer only ONE of these two questions.

Part C also presents two standard free-response questions (FRQs). Again, choose and answer ONE of these questions. A sample free-response question is provided at the end of Chapter 5.

Here are some tips for doing well on the essay section of the test:

Answer in Your Own Order

You do not have to answer the essays in the order in which they appear. When you open your essay test packet, scan all the questions and choose the essay for which you have the most ready response. Beginning with your strongest area will help boost your confidence.

Read Critically

Before you start writing, read and decode the essay prompt carefully. What is it asking? Is there more than one part to the question? Read the prompt with your pen in your hand. Underline, circle, and make notations.

Organize and Structure Your Essay

For each type of essay question, be sure to:

- have a relevant thesis or position
- support that thesis with historical evidence
- address all parts of the question
- analyze and explain—don't summarize

Don't include personal opinions in the essay. The reader is looking for your grasp of the history itself and your ability to write about it.

Stick to the topic and time period. Giving historical information before or after the period of the essay will not win you any points.

A longer essay is not necessarily better, but it takes more than a paragraph or two to merit a good score. As a general rule, aim for five parts: an introduction, three body paragraphs, and a conclusion. Another good rule of thumb is one body paragraph for each portion of the essay prompt.

Write It Out

Write as neatly and as legibly as you can. Test scorers understand that your essays are drafts. Cross-outs, inserted lines with arrows, and other working thoughts are acceptable as long as they are clear. However, avoid using abbreviations, shorthand symbols (such as & or @) or texting spelling. If the reader does not understand the symbol or word, he or she will ignore it, and you might not gain a point.

> ▶ AP EXPERT TIP
>
> When composing your essay, start with your most important information. That way, if you run out of time while you're writing, your key points are already in the essay.

You must write an *essay* for each question. Bullet notes, diagrams, or lists of information are not considered essay format and will be ignored by the reader.

Pace Yourself

A total of 130 minutes, or 2 hours and 10 minutes, is allotted for reading, organizing, and writing all three questions. The first 15 minutes are a mandatory reading period. Your proctor will *not* tell you to move from one essay to the next—you must do this on your own.

Essay Type	Budgeted Time
Part A: DBQ	45 min (includes 15 min. reading period)
Part B: FRQ	35 min.
Part C: FRQ	35 min.

The DBQ essay counts for 45 percent of your essay grade. The two FRQs count for 55 percent. You do not want to rush through the essays too quickly, and you do not want to run out of time. Partial essays do not receive high scores. Bring a watch, and budget your time for each essay.

Practice essay questions, with scoring guides and strategies for each question type, are provided at the ends of chapters 3 and 5.

> ▶ AP EXPERT TIPS
>
> 1. Remember things like Pacing, Process of Elimination, and Reading Critically.
> 2. Know how to manage your stress. You can beat anxiety the same way you can beat the exam—by knowing what to expect beforehand and developing strategies to deal with it.
> 3. Take Kaplan's practice tests to learn your test-taking strengths and weaknesses. Knowing these will allow you to focus on your problem areas as you prepare for test day.
> 4. Get organized! Make a study schedule between now and test day and give yourself plenty of time to prepare. Waiting until the last minute to cram info is not only unwise but exhausting.
> 5. Make a test day game plan. Have everything you need to bring to the exam ready the night before. Make it a priority to eat a good breakfast. Avoid an overindulgence of caffeine. Read something to warm up your brain. And finally, get to the test site early.

CHAPTER 1

Pre-Revolutionary Times: 1492–1783

❯❯ DISCOVERING AND SETTLING THE NEW WORLD: 1492–1700

The New World

LATE 1400S AND 1500S, NORTH AMERICA

Scattered Native American communities, many with subsistence lifestyles and many of them matrilineal, dotted the continent. There were language and cultural differences among tribes and not much intertribal cooperation or cohesiveness among the various native peoples.

Europe

THOUGHT AND RELIGION

The European Renaissance began in the fourteenth century and fed the search for knowledge and dominion as a spirit of **scientific inquiry** emerged. A series of rifts among Christians led to **Protestantism**. Inspired by the protests of the German monk **Martin Luther**, the movement now known as the **Protestant Reformation** swept across Northern European countries that had once been loyal to the Roman Catholic Church. This occurred after the publication of **Luther's *95 Theses*** in 1517. Luther protested the Catholic Church's belief that one could not find redemption without doing "good works" and following Church sacraments; he proposed that salvation was to be gained through faith alone. Thanks to the advent of the printing press, Luther's views circulated rapidly, and to the dismay of the Catholic Church, Lutheran Protestantism spread. This gave rise to a series of religious wars that affected Northern and Western Europe from 1521 to 1648.

> ▶ **AP EXPERT TIP**
>
> Throughout your review of U.S. History, try to keep in mind the helpful acronym PERSIA (Political, Economic, Religious, Social, Intellectual and Arts) and look for these currents existing or emerging during various periods.

Another form of Protestantism called **Calvinism** arose from the ideas of a middle-class, French-born intellectual named **John Calvin,** who elaborated on some of Luther's ideas but did not agree with others. In Calvin's view, one could not get into heaven through good deeds and faith alone. Calvinists believed in the inherent wickedness of human nature and in **predestination**. According to this belief, some people (**the elect**) were born to find salvation through a conversion experience that revealed God's will, while others were destined to a life that led to eternal damnation. In their view, strict leadership was needed to keep people from sin.

The **Roman Catholic Church** sought to gain new followers to replace the ones it had lost by converting non-Christians in distant lands. Spain's Catholic rulers **Ferdinand & Isabella** expelled the Moors (Muslims) from Spain and began an aggressive exploration of new lands, as well as the conquest of known ones. Their fight to gain dominion far and wide was done in the name of the Roman Catholic Church.

EXPLORATION AND CONQUEST

In the name of spreading the faith, nations and religious entities set out to claim parts of the newly discovered lands and gain power and riches through them.

Via the **Treaty of Tordesillas,** 1494, Spain and Portugal divided the lands Columbus had discovered between them-selves. Spain's rulers, starting with Ferdinand and Isabella, then sent explorers to the New World to claim areas, enslave the natives, and gain treasure. These **conquistadores** included **Vasco Núñez de Balboa, Juan Ponce de León, Francisco Pizarro**, and **Hernan Cortés**. The Spanish operated under the **encomienda**, by which Spaniards who were given land in conquered areas of the New World were obligated to care for the natives (now, essentially, their slaves) there. South and Central America were dominated by Spain, which also ruled Florida and other parts of present Southwest United States, including California.

Arriving in 1524, the French established themselves in North America in the land that is presently **Canada**, as well as the upper northeastern United States. They created vast trade networks, which extended **down the Mississippi** all the way to **New Orleans**, by doing business (mainly in beaver pelts) with Native Americans. The French also brought European diseases, guns, and alcohol to the natives and contributed to the rise of intertribal warfare.

England sent explorers to claim land and establish settlements. In 1585 **Sir Walter Raleigh** established the colony of **Roanoke** off the coast of present-day North Carolina, which mysteriously vanished later. In 1607, the **Virginia Company** was set up to establish a permanent colony in America and authorized **Captain John Smith** to organize the **Jamestown Colony** on the James River. It established English settlers who were accustomed to having rights by giving them a charter providing them with the same privileges as they had enjoyed as citizens of Britain.

In the early 1600s, the **New England colonies (Massachusetts, Connecticut, Rhode Island, and New Hampshire)** were settled by a number of Calvinists who were known as the **Puritans.**

❯❯ THE ATLANTIC WORLD: 1600–1750

Religion and Colonization

The **Church of England (Anglican Church)** had been founded in 1534 by **King Henry VIII** after the Roman Catho-lic Church under **Pope Clement** would not allow him to divorce his wife, **Catherine of Aragon.** Calling himself **the Defender of the Faith,** King Henry had broken away from Roman Catholicism and created the Anglican Church. Though this new Anglican faith permitted divorce, the Church of England held on to most of the ceremony and rega-lia of the Catholic Church.

Many years later, during the reign of **King James I**, a number of Anglicans, influenced by the teachings of John Calvin, formed a sect known as the **Puritans** and sought to **purify** the Anglican Church by ridding it of the regalia and ceremony it still had in common with Roman Catholicism. **Separatist Puritans** known as **Pilgrims** wanted to form a new church that would be independent of the monarchy. **Nonseparatist Puritans** wanted to reform the Anglican Church from within. King James, who viewed the Puritans as a threat to his power, was determined to drive them all out of his kingdom and oppressed them.

The New England Colonies

THE PILGRIMS OF PLYMOUTH

The Pilgrims were Puritan separatists who wished to form a new church. Persecuted in England, they sought a life elsewhere, agreeing to go to the New World with the condition that they would spend their first seven years working for the **Virginia Company** (in exchange for a share of the profits they gained during that time). In **1620**, the group boarded a ship known as the *Mayflower* and set sail for **Virginia**. Unable to get to Virginia, the ship landed in **Plymouth Bay**. Once on dry land, the Pilgrims chose a site for their settlement and created it in what is now known as **Massachusetts**.

While on the high seas, the Pilgrims had drafted the *Mayflower Compact*, an agreement by which they agreed to administer their colony by means of a **secular** body. Although the concepts set forth in this document would form the basis of our country's later ideas of majority rule and the separation of church and state, religion remained the most important element in the lives of these Pilgrims.

THE PURITANS OF THE MASSACHUSETTS BAY COLONY

Led by their governor, **John Winthrop,** who was also a Puritan minister, these nonseparatist settlers led **the Great Migration** to the Massachusetts Bay Colony in the 1630s. In his sermon **Model of Christian Charity**, Winthrop vowed to make their new home a "city upon a hill" that would inspire the Christian world.

In the **Cambridge Agreement** of 1629, the colony's stockholders agreed to let the emigrating members establish their government in America instead of England, leading to a theocracy. Only freemen—male stockholders who were members of the **Congregational Church**—could vote. To become church members, men and women had to demonstrate publicly that they had had a conversion experience and led a life of piety. By the 1660s, few people could do this, so church membership was declining. To remedy this, the **Halfway Covenant** of 1662 allowed partial members who had been baptized but couldn't prove conversion to baptize their children, who might become full members if they themselves could later prove conversion.

In 1692, a few young girls in Salem, Massachusetts, took sick and began to have strange convulsions. One was the daughter of a former merchant from Barbados, hired in Salem as a minister, who owned an Indian slave that spoke of voodoo. The daughter and her playmates accused the slave and members of the church of witchcraft. In the mass hysteria that followed, 20 people were executed, and the traditional Puritan clergy fell into disrepute. This is referred to as **the Salem Witch Trials.**

Non-Puritans and Dissenters were punished and often banished from the colony. **Anne Hutchinson**, who preached **antinomianism** (a belief that since God's chosen people are predestined for Heaven they do not need to obey God's or man's laws) was banished for her beliefs and for holding prayer meetings.

Some dissenters, when banished, left with followers and formed their own colonies. **Roger Williams**, a minister from Salem who advocated a complete separation of church and state, believed that the biddings of conscience stood above civil or church laws. He also held that colonists had no right to live on lands unlawfully taken from Native Americans. After banishment, he and his followers established the settlement of **Providence**, in what was later the colony of **Rhode Island.**

The Quakers, who believed no clergy was necessary for one to experience God and Jesus Christ (one's **"inner light"**) were also banished. Several were executed, and several others joined **William Penn** of England, who founded **Penn's Woods (Pennsylvania)**.

SEEDS OF AUTONOMY

In **1639**, Connecticut settlers drafted a sort of constitution called the **Fundamental Orders**, which called for the power of government to be drawn from the governed.

From 1642–1651, when England was preoccupied with a civil war, the British colonies in the New World existed in a state of **salutary neglect** by their motherland. This hands-off policy led the colonies to become increasingly self-reliant, and the distance between the ideologies of the mother country and her colonies widened. In **1643**, under frequent attack from Native American tribes, the New England colonies formed the **New England Confederation**, which provided for the collective security of its member settlements. Later, in **1686**, **King James II** was angered by what he saw as the political and economic insolence of the New England colonies, who were behaving as if they did not exist purely for the economic benefit of England. He established the **Dominion of New England** to bring them under stricter control. In addition, starting in 1651, a series of Navigation Acts restricted colonial trade with countries other than England and required goods to be transported in British ships. This inspired quiet rebellion in the colonies, and smuggling and black markets grew.

The Middle Colonies

New York, Pennsylviania, New Jersey, and **Delaware** were economically, socially and religiously much more diverse than the New England or Southern colonies. New York came into being when the English took over the **Dutch** colony of **New Netherlands**. Its principal city of **New Amsterdam** had originally been founded as a fur trading center by the **Dutch West India Company** in **1623**. After a series of misfortunes that included repeated attacks by surrounding Native tribes, Swedish incursions into the territory, and finally, conquest by the English, New Netherlands acquired its present name when **King Charles II** granted it to his brother, the **Duke of York**. As an English colony, New York enjoyed more democracy than most other British colonies, but it had a social structure based on land distribution that resembled that of feudal England.

New Jersey (1664), Pennsylvania (1681, William Penn's "Holy Experiment") and **Delaware (1703)** were all havens for Quakers. Established from within the New World, these three colonies were liberal states that lured a wide array of potential settlers with the promise of land, religious freedom, and democracy. Nonviolence (including nonviolent resistance) was practiced. Known for business acumen, the Quakers maintained good relations with surrounding Native American tribes and built vast trade networks.

Foundations of Chesapeake and Southern Economies

THE HEADRIGHT SYSTEM

This system was designed to attract new immigrants to work the land by granting 50 acres of land to any white individual willing to pay his passage from England. If an individual was willing to pay for another person to come over and work on the land, he received 50 acres for each individual he brought over. The person whose passage had been paid was obliged to work in servitude, usually for seven years, under a contract called an **indenture**. After the term of **indentured servitude** was over, the former servant would be free to make his or her own way. Former identured servants often moved into unsettled lands, necessitating a new supply of laborers to work the old land and even more laborers to work the additional newly settled lands.

SLAVERY

Before 1660, many Africans arriving in Virginia were considered indentured servants and set free after they had paid back their debt. However, in 1662, the Virginia House of Burgesses passed a series of laws distinguishing whites from blacks. From that day on, black servants and their offspring were considered lifelong slaves. As the number of white indentured servants decreased, more and more African slaves were brought to serve as labor in their places.

THE CHESAPEAKE COLONIES

Captain John Smith brought the first British settlers to the **Chesapeake Bay Region** in **1607**. Initially established by the Virginia Company as an economic venture, the colony of Virginia acquired a royal charter from **King James I** in **1624** in the expectation that it would provide gold, religious influence, and glory to England.

Under the leadership of **John Rolph**, tobacco farming was introduced to the Chesapeake Bay area and soon became the area's top cash crop. Because tobacco had to be grown on a grand scale to be profitable and required much acreage and many workers, the region needed more laborers than its own population could provide. Because there were relatively few women in the population, the birth rate remained low while the death rate (amplified by the preponderance of disease and unfriendly climate conditions) stayed high. The labor shortage gave rise to the **headright system**, **indentured servitude**, and **slavery**. The **plantation system** developed because of the needs connected with tobacco farming.

In **1634**, King Charles I divided the Virginia Colony and gave one part to **Lord Baltimore (George Calvert).** The king established the **proprietary colony of Maryland** in order to have more control over its administration and protect his influence in the Chesapeake region. He directed Lord Baltimore to create a profitable colony that would also provide haven for Catholics; Lord Baltimore passed away before this had been done. The colony was then in the hands of Lord Baltimore's son, Cecil Calvert, the second Lord Baltimore, who established Maryland. Because Protestant farmers immigrating to Maryland were making the prospect of its becoming a sanctuary for Catholics less likely, Calvert persuaded the legislative assembly to pass an **Act of Toleration** in **1649**. This act, which guaranteed religious freedom to all Christians, also stipulated that anyone who denied Christ's divinity should be put to death.

In **Virginia**, indentured servants who had gained their freedom usually tilled land in the backwoods regions of Virginia, where they were vulnerable to attacks from Native Americans. Politics in the colony tended to favor large plantation owners. Sir William Berkeley, governor of the Virginia Colony, further angered these poor farmers by maintaining good relations with the native tribes while failing to protect the poor Virginians. In 1676, a young member of the House of Burgesses named **Nathaniel Bacon** led a citizens' militia that raided native villages, slaughtered the inhabitants, defeated Berkeley's forces, and set fire to Jamestown. **Bacon's Rebellion** was finally crushed after its leader died of dysentery, but it had spotlighted social divisions, colonial resistance, and, especially, the difficulty of controlling former indentured servants. One result of this was an increasing demand for black slaves.

The Southern Colonies

Georgia, founded and chartered in **1733** by **James Oglethorpe**, was the last of the British colonies. English debtors crowding jails in London were transported to this colony. Georgia served as a buffer between the valued Carolina plantations and Florida, then a Spanish possession.

THE RESTORATION COLONIES

North Carolina and **South Carolina** were called Restoration Colonies because they were established (along with New York and Pennsylvania to the north) after the English throne was restored to Charles II in **1660**. Originally established to provide food for West Indian sugar plantations, their plantations grew rice, the favored cash crop, and indigo.

South Carolina, whose influence was centered in Charleston, became a relatively aristocratic region of the American colonies. The Carolinas first imported slaves from Barbados, institutionalizing black slavery.

Colonial Autonomy after James II

Also of significance to the colonies in the late 1600s was England's **"Glorious Revolution"** during which James II, whose repressive measures against the Puritans and efforts to limit colonial self-governance had not endeared him to the colonists, was replaced by Queen Mary and her husband, William of Orange, in **1688**. However, it soon became clear that Britain still wanted to restrict colonial self-rule. Colonial uprisings followed by British-led suppressions only widened the rift between the colonists and their mother country, England.

The Southwest

Unrest also arose in the Spanish-held territories to the west. In **1675**, the Spanish governor of New Mexico had begun banning Pueblo Indian religious practices, as well as whipping Indians accused of being witches, sparking the **Pueblo Revolt of 1680** (also called Popé's Rebellion). This occurred in response to the flogging of an influential Hopi who had opposed colonial rule. In the course of an organized attack, the Indians killed over 400 Spaniards, destroyed all the buildings they had erected, and took over the governor's residence. A few Spanish survivors managed to flee to Santa Fe and make their way from there to El Paso, but Spain was not able to reclaim its New Mexico colony for nearly 50 years.

❷ LIFE IN THE COLONIES

Social Structure

With fewer than 300,000 inhabitants in 1700, by 1775 the population of the English-American colonies grew to almost 2.5 million (20 percent of this representing African slaves on Southern plantations).

Just as in England, colonial social structure was **stratified**. In New England's Puritan society, wealth and success were viewed as signs of membership in God's **elect**, while in the South, leaders known as **"Cavaliers"** came in to build a society that honored its landed aristocracy. In New England and the South, the gap between rich and poor also widened as new affluent settlers arrived and the South's plantation economy continued to grow. In comparison, the Middle Colonies were more diverse and tolerant and less socially rigid.

Ninety percent of colonists were involved in agriculture, and the family was at the center of economic and social well-being. Since children served as farmhands, people married young and had as many children as possible. Men labored outside the home; women reared the children and cared for the homestead. Women had few rights but were protected under law from abuse by their husbands.

Under **King James II** and with the **Dominion of New England** in 1686, **mercantilism** (the concept that colonies exist only to supply raw materials and a market to the mother country) held sway. However, in spite of the **Navigation Acts**, which weren't heavily enforced anyway, the colonists developed unsanctioned markets. One was the rum-running **Triangular Trade**, through which New England goods were exchanged with the Caribbean for molasses, which was used to make rum, which was then traded for slaves in Africa.

Agriculture and light manufacturing in the Middle Colonies yielded products for markets primarily in the West Indies. Tobacco was the cash crop of the Chesapeake (Virginia and Maryland), while Carolina and Georgia specialized in rice and indigo, all of which were traded with England and the West Indies for manufactured goods and slaves.

During the mid-1700s, when many colonists lost touch with Puritanism's Calvinist ideas and settlers on the frontier had little access to churches, a wave of preachers who delivered sermons emphasizing personal inspiration and emotional connection to God held large revival meetings in tents on the outskirts of towns, sparking the **Great Awakening**. **New Light** preacher **Jonathan Edwards,** famous for the sermon "**Sinners in the Hands of an Angry God,**" started the movement in 1734, telling people to pray for salvation or face **fire and brimstone**. George Whitefield, who helped found Methodism in America, was perhaps the most famous preacher of the time. Impacting all strata of society, the movement had a democratizing effect on society, led to the birth of the Baptist and Methodist sects, and overrode the old intellectual faiths with a new emotionalism. Universities such as Dartmouth, Rutgers, and Princeton were formed to educate New Light ministers.

❯❯ THE EVE OF THE REVOLUTION

In **1713,** the **Treaty of Utrecht** ushered in many years of peace in Europe. During the time, under England's Prime Minister **Robert Walpole**, the colonies were treated with **salutary neglect**. Besides providing opportunities for trade and offering protection when needed, England let the colonies govern themselves and develop their own economic networks and ideologies. However, in 1754 **the French and Indian War,** a New World conflict sparked by European territorial ambitions, led to the outbreak of Europe's **Seven Years' War** in **1756** at the same time as it encouraged the British colonies to organize in a manner that would one day support a revolt against the motherland.

Hostilities were focused on a French foothold in the Ohio Valley. In 1754, the French were fortifying the region in the hopes of halting British expansion westward, while the British aspired to drive the French out of North America. As France's **Fort Duquesne** (now Pittsburgh) neared completion, Lt. Colonel **George Washington** was sent by Virginia's governor to stop the work. After an initial victory, he was driven back and forced to surrender by the French and their Native American allies. As these events unfolded, British officials convened a meeting called the **Albany Congress**. There important colonial tradesmen, led by a Pennsylvania newspaperman named **Benjamin Franklin**, devised the **Albany Plan of Union**, calling for a confederation of colonies able to defend themselves from European and Native American attackers. To promote this, Franklin's paper, the *Pennsylvania Gazette*, ran a cartoon called "**Join, or Die.**" However, the plan was not accepted because the colonies felt it was too restrictive while the British felt it allowed for too much power in colonial hands.

Under **Prime Minister William Pitt**, the British devoted resources to conquering French Canada, taking Quebec in 1759 and Montreal in 1760. With the **Peace of Paris**, signed in 1763, England gained French Canada and Spanish Florida and became North America's dominant power. However, a gulf grew between England and its colonies. The English felt that the colonies couldn't protect themselves, while the colonists, cheered by their successes, felt differently and did not like the way the British military had treated the colonial militia. The war had left England in debt. English citizens were paying higher taxes and higher prices as a result of war, but the colonists did not want to pay for England's wars.

In 1763, Native Americans in the Ohio Valley refused to hand over conquered lands to the British because the British had treated them so harshly. During **Pontiac's Rebellion,** Ottowan **Chief Pontiac** attacked many colonial settlements, doing much damage. After 18 months, regular British forces were called in, and the rebellion was subdued. To make peace with the Native American tribes and avoid similar future situations, King George III signed **the Proclamation of 1763**, which pledged that American colonists would not settle west of the Appalachian Mountains. Angered by this, most colonists ignored it.

Burdened by its war debt, England abandoned its policy of salutary neglect and imposed the **Sugar Acts of 1764**, which taxed sweeteners, particularly the molasses the colonies used when defying British rules to make and trade in rum. It also passed **the Quartering Act,** requiring colonists to give room and board to British soldiers. These were laxly enforced. However, when **the Stamp Act,** authorized by **Prime Minister George Grenville** to tax directly all paper used in the colonies and meant to raise revenues to build a new colonial army, went into effect in 1765, colonists were enraged. In Virginia, a young lawyer named **Patrick Henry** introduced the Stamp Act Resolves in the House of Burgesses, which denied Parliament's attempt to engage in taxation without representation. In Massachusetts, James Otis gathered representatives of 9 of the 13 colonies, who met as the **Stamp Act Congress** in New York. They decided that England could levy **external taxes** (duties on traded goods), but that **internal taxes** (levied directly on a region's people) could only be authorized by locally elected officials. Grenville replied that the colonists did have (virtual) representation in Parliament.

The colonists were angry. They boycotted British goods. The **Sons and Daughters of Liberty** intimidated tax collectors and burned stamp warehouses. Because the boycotts hurt England, the Stamp Act was cancelled, but it was replaced by the **Declaratory Act**, which maintained the crown's right to impose future taxes on the colonies. The new chancellor of the exchequer, Charles Townshend, instituted the **Townshend Acts**, passed in **1767**, a series of acts which, among other revenue-raising schemes, placed duties on imports—an "external tax." It also re-established **Writs of Assistance**, which allowed customs officials to search homes, businesses, and warehouses for smuggled goods without a warrant from a judge. In **the Massachusetts Circular Letter**, distributed throughout the colonies, **Samuel Adams** argued that there was no difference between external and internal taxes. This sparked new boycotts of British goods, leading to the repeal of the Townshend Acts.

Though Boston remained generally calm, in 1770, one angry crowd that threw rocks at the custom house provoked guards to fire on the protestors, killing some and injuring others (**Boston Massacre**). Egged on by Sam Adams, **Committees of Correspondence** circulated letters protesting British policies. The destruction of the British warship *Gaspée,* which had been commissioned to capture vessels carrying smuggled goods to the colonies, was celebrated.

Because colonists were so wary of revenue collection efforts, passage of the innocuous **Tea Act**, which forced colonists to buy East India Company Tea at bargain prices to bail out the company, prompted some colonists, dressed as Native Americans, to board a ship in Boston Harbor and dump its cargo of tea overboard. In order to punish colonists for the **Boston Tea Party,** Parliament passed the **Coercive Acts**. These closed Boston Harbor until the tea was paid for; revoked the charter of Massachusetts and put the colony under control of the crown; and expanded the scope of the Quartering Acts, which housed British soldiers in private homes. In **1774**, Parliament also passed the **Quebec Act,** which allowed the former French region to be self-sufficient and expanded its borders, depriving Ohio River Valley colonists of potential lands. The colonists were particularly angered that the act let Quebecers practice Catholicism freely, and they named all these acts the **Intolerable Acts**.

Americans were affected by British philosopher **John Locke's** theory of natural rights, which disputed the absolute and divine rights of kings and asserted that sovereignty was derived from the will of the governed; accordingly, the governed should rebel against governments that fail to protect the natural rights of life, liberty, and property. These and other Enlightenment teachings influenced many colonists, who began to emphasize the concept of reason over emotion, and set the stage for revolutionary thinking.

❯❯ THE AMERICAN REVOLUTION

The Colonies Organize

The colonies organized quickly in response to the Intolerable Acts. In September 1774, 12 of the 13 colonies sent representatives to the **First Continental Congress** in Philadelphia, which then sent a **Declaration of Rights and Grievances** to the king, urging him to correct wrongs done to the colonies while acknowledging Parliament's right to regulate commerce. The Congress also created the **Association**, which called for the creation of **boycott committees** that could pressure Britain economically, throughout the colonies, and the Congress planned to reconvene later if its grievances were not addressed. England did not want to reinforce the Congress's claims to legitimacy by responding to its demands and did not do so.

General Thomas Gage, the English governor of Massachusetts, ordered his soldiers to seize the colonists' arms and arrest rebels in Concord. However, some members of the colonial militia, the **Minutemen**, who had been forewarned, assembled in Lexington to stop the British **redcoats**. There, in April of 1775, they fired **"the shot heard round the world"** that started the American Revolution. Outnumbered by the British, the Minutemen were forced to retreat. Though the British were able to march to Concord, they were then forced back and had to retreat to Boston, losing about 250 men in the process.

The **Second Continental Congress** met in May of 1775, with representatives from all 13 colonies in attendance. There was no easy agreement among them. The New England colonies were most radical, and many called for independence, while the Middle Colonies wanted to reopen negotiations with Britain. However, all knew they needed to arrive at consensus. Northern delegates shrewdly agreed to put **George Washington** of Virginia in charge of the Continental Army, because his leadership would ensure Southern support of the war effort. The Congress drew up the **Declaration of the Causes and Necessities of Taking Up Arms** to form a professional colonial army while urging King George II to reconsider colonial grievances.

> ❯ **AP EXPERT TIP**
>
> Create acronyms or other mnemonic devices to jog your memory. For example, SADTWITS can help you remember the American Revolution:
>
> **S** = Sugar Act
> **A** = Admiralty Courts
> **D** = Declaratory Act
> **T** = Townshend Acts
> **W** = Writs of Assistance
> **I** = Intolerable Acts
> **T** = Tea Act
> **S** = Stamp Act

The Rift Between England and Her Colonies Widens

On June 17, 1775, the British and colonists fought for the stronghold of **Bunker Hill**. Though the Americans lost this tactical site, they inflicted major casualties on their powerful adversary. The king then declared war by announcing that the colonies were in rebellion, and he hired Hessian mercenaries (from Germany and famous for ruthlessness) to invade the colonies.

England had money, the world's most powerful navy, and ample recruits to fight its war. However, since England's army was far from home and had to function during lag times when orders for new munitions and reinforcements were relayed to England, they were not invulnerable. Though the colonists had superb military leadership and a much greater familiarity with the terrain of battle than their adversaries, they struggled with infighting among the colonies, a demoralizing lack of funds to pay their soldiers, and shrinking supplies.

In July of 1775, the Congress sought to avoid total war by sending England the **Olive Branch Petition**, which reasserted colonial loyalty to the crown and asked the king to intervene with parliament on behalf of the colonies. Once again though, the king refused to recognize the legitimacy of the Congress.

The Declaration of Independence Initiates War

In January of 1776, a recent English immigrant to the colonies named **Thomas Paine** published a pamphlet called *Common Sense*, using **John Locke's natural rights** philosophy to support the idea of rebellion against British oppression because common sense could not allow the continuation of these injustices.

The Second Continental Congress

Congress took its stand after a year of deliberation. On June 7, 1776, a call for a resolution declaring the colonies independent of Britain went up. A committee, which included **Thomas Jefferson** and four other delegates, was chosen to draft the **Declaration of Independence,** which officially broke the colonies' connection with England and formed a new country. The document's preamble reflected Locke's natural rights philosophy. The Congress also drafted a national constitution called the **Articles of Confederation**, which was then accepted and sent to the states for ratification in 1777. The Articles provided for a central government with a unicameral legislative branch, and it required a unanimous vote to amend the Articles and a two-thirds majority vote to pass laws. It specified a central government that could wage war, make treaties, and borrow money to pay debts, and it established clear policies regarding the settlement and statehood of newly acquired lands to the west. Before ratification was to occur, however, coastal and inland states had to resolve their differences over the administration of westward lands.

Colonial citizens were not of one view, however. About a third of them were aligned with the fight for independence (the **patriots),** a third remained loyal to England (**Loyalists** or **Tories**), while a third remained disinterested. The Loyalists usually belonged to the older elite of the Middle or Southern colonies, while the Patriots, mostly New Englanders or Virginians, volunteered for the army, alternating between short tours of military duty and brief shifts spent fulfilling the duties of home, farm, and other occupations.

The War Heats Up

Though General Washington's army had an unhappy beginning, losing New York City in 1776, it then won small battles in New Jersey in 1777. However, it was not Washington, but generals **Benedict Arnold** and **Horatio Gates** who won the **Battle of Saratoga**, the most important battle of the war, in October of **1777.** The victory gave the French the reassurance they needed to enter the war on behalf of the revolutionaries. Monetary aid from France, which now assisted the enemy of their enemy, England, turned the tide for the Continental army. States continued to wrangle over some terms of the Articles of Confederation, and colonies were also drafting and ratifying their own state constitutions. By 1777 all but three of the colonies had done so, as they attempted to balance law and order and protect natural rights. Most provided suffrage for landholding male citizens and protection of basic rights. In 1781, the Articles of Confederation were finally ratified, with all 13 states signing on.

The War Winds Down

Washington's forces survived a horribly cold winter at **Valley Forge**, Pennsylvania, in 1777–78, and they were able to win battles against the depleted British forces as they marched to Virginia. In **1781** the last major battle of the Revolution, the **Battle of Yorktown**, pitted Washington's army, aided by French forces, against the British. The English, under **General Cornwallis**, had to surrender. Economically hard-pressed English citizens voted the Tory government out in favor of a Whig government interested in ending the war with America. In **1783** the British and Americans met in Paris. As a result of their negotiations, a peace treaty called the **Treaty of Paris** was signed. England formally recognized the United States as a country with boundaries stretching west to the Mississippi River and allowed the United States to retain fishing rights in Newfoundland. The Americans agreed to repay debts owed to

British merchants and promised not to punish any Loyalists who chose to remain in the United States. Still, 60,000 to 80,000 Loyalists chose to leave.

New Ordinances

The fledgling country passed new laws and policies. **The Land Ordinance of 1785** set up orderly settlement of the Northwest; it stipulated that new townships of six miles square had to set aside a parcel of land for public education, and that the proceeds from sales of public lands would be used to pay off the national debt. **The Northwest Ordinance of 1787** permitted territories to apply for statehood when populated by at least 60,000 settlers and specified that, if Congress granted statehood to a region, the new state would have the same status as older states. It also banned slavery north of the Ohio River. To reduce the risk of tyranny and government abuse of power, the government had not been given the power to tax its citizens or enforce its own laws. The nation could request taxes from the states, but it could not enforce tax collection. Without tax revenue, the government could not pay the large war debts it had promised to settle. Broken trade relationships and a depreciated currency weakened the United States. The possibility of being invaded by Spain or England loomed large.

❯ SHAYS' REBELLION AND ITS AFTERMATH

Shays' Rebellion began in the summer of 1786 when a band of farmers in Massachusetts led by Daniel Shays protested oppressive taxes, debtors' prisons, and the lack of valuable currency by demanding restitution and tax relief. The situation escalated when a mob seized the state arsenal in January of 1787. Though quickly quelled by the state militia, this seemingly minor insurrection signaled that the country had not yet enabled the states to protect the rights and liberties of citizens. When a convention held in Annapolis, Maryland, in 1786 to deal with the regulation of commerce drew only five delegates, political heavyweights **James Madison** and **Alexander Hamilton** called for another convention to be held in Philadelphia. Though originally intended as a meeting to revise the Articles of Confederation, the tone soon shifted. The product that came out of the gathering that began in **May of 1787** has since determined its name. **The Constitutional Convention** would launch the next stage of U.S. history.

THINGS TO REMEMBER

TERMS

Elect	Separatists	headright system	"Sinners in the Hands
ecomienda	Pilgrims	proprietary colonies	of an Angry God"
The Church of England	nonseparatists	indentured servants	salutary neglect
Puritans	Quakers	New Light preachers	writs of assistance
New England	antinomianism	stratification	
Confederation	plantation system	mercantilism	

PEOPLE

John Calvin	Roger Williams	William and Mary	William Pitt
Martin Luther	John Rolfe	Jonathan Edwards	Sons and Daughters
John Smith	Lord Baltimore	George Whitefield	of Liberty
John Winthrop	Sir William Berkeley	Benjamin Franklin	Daniel Shays
Anne Hutchinson	Nathaniel Bacon	John Locke	

THINGS TO REMEMBER

EVENTS

Protestant Reformation	Pueblo Revolt	French and Indian War	Boston Tea Party
Great Migration	Glorious Revolution	Pontiac's Rebellion	First Continental Congress
Holy Experiment	Triangular Trade	Stamp Act Congress	Second Continental
Bacon's Rebellion	Great Awakening	Boston Massacre	Congress

PLACES

Roanoake	Virginia Company	Salem	Jamestown

DOCUMENTS

Treaty of Tordesillas	Peace of Paris	Massachusetts Circular	Olive Branch Petition
Mayflower Compact	Proclamation of 1763	Letter	Common Sense
Halfway Covenant	Sugar Acts	Coercive Acts	Northwest Ordinance
Dominion of New England	Quartering Act	Quebec Act	of 1787
Act of Toleration	Declaratory Act	Intolerable Acts	
Fundamental Orders	Townshend Acts	Declaration of Rights	
Albany Plan of Union	Tea Act	and Grievances	

Practice Section

1. The biggest reason that Europeans were able to overpower inhabitants in the New World was the

   (A) compliance of the tribes that were confronted.
   (B) unsophisticated and incompetent social structure of Native Americans.
   (C) lack of healthy tribal populations.
   (D) differences of population and cultural arrangements among tribes.
   (E) the enthusiasm of the natives to adopt Christianity.

2. Puritans were different from Pilgrims because they

   (A) were not Protestant.
   (B) continued to be participants in the Church of England.
   (C) accepted the idea of antinomianism.
   (D) were not persecuted in England.
   (E) spoke in tongues while in congregation.

3. The Maryland Act of Toleration

   (A) was created by King James II.
   (B) permitted Jews to perform religious ceremonies freely.
   (C) removed all religions but Catholicism from the colony.
   (D) accepted Catholicism, but refused religions that did not support Jesus.
   (E) was eliminated by Parliament.

4. The Triangular Trade was created in the New World to

   (A) evade the Navigation Acts.
   (B) conform to mercantilism.
   (C) supply raw materials to the mother country.
   (D) preserve the plantation structure of the South.
   (E) generate a sustained money income.

5. The Great Awakening was culturally important because it

   (A) united Protestants under one denomination.
   (B) further separated the wealthy from the impoverished.
   (C) included all colonists regardless of social class.
   (D) led to a decline in church membership.
   (E) detracted from the insistence on higher education.

6. The Albany Plan for Union was discarded by the colonies because

   (A) it did not offer defense against Native Americans.
   (B) too much power was given to a central government.
   (C) there was not enough self-government for individual colonies.
   (D) it acknowledged French claims to the Ohio Valley.
   (E) the House of Burgesses desired to uphold control.

7. According to the British, the Proclamation of 1763 was created to

   (A) defend the colonists from Native American assaults.

   (B) develop colonial settlements in the west.

   (C) initiate a war between colonists and the Native Americans.

   (D) require colonials to pay taxes.

   (E) display the authority of the British sovereignty.

8. The Committees of Correspondence

   (A) smuggled tea, glass, and silk into the colonies.

   (B) spread propaganda about British injustice throughout the colonies.

   (C) led to the *Gaspée* incident.

   (D) were acclaimed by the British government.

   (E) persuaded colonists to pay taxes to sustain the war endeavors.

9. The Enlightenment was significant in the colonies because

   (A) colonists perceived a kinship with their English counterparts.

   (B) it unified the colonies in a common struggle.

   (C) religion replaced reason in terms of political ideas.

   (D) its ideas supported colonial rebellion against Britain.

   (E) a renewed religious zeal extended across the colonies.

10. The First Continental Congress was called to

   (A) discuss suitable forms of colonial protest.

   (B) arrange a military power.

   (C) claim independence from Britain.

   (D) discipline colonies that failed to abide by the Quebec Act.

   (E) form a legislative framework for new territories.

Answers and Explanations

1. D

Native Americans were spread out across the Americas with sometimes hundreds of miles between settlements. Tribes usually did not share a common religion or language, which also contributed to their inability to join together to repel the Europeans from their homeland.

2. B

The Pilgrims were referred to as separatists; they felt they had to leave the Church of England to escape a life they did not support. The Puritans, on the other hand, trusted that they needed to stay in the Church in order to serve as spiritual examples and purify the Church from within. However, once the Puritans left England for North America, they no longer continued to be active in the Church of England.

3. D

The Maryland Act of Toleration gave Catholics a safe refuge in Maryland, but it did not allow others, such as Jews, to practice their religion openly.

4. A

In an effort to become more autonomous, the colonies engaged in the illegal Triangular Trade. This trade network was established to avoid the limitations of the Navigation Acts and mercantilism.

5. C

The Great Awakening touched colonists from all classes and backgrounds, unifying them. Protestant churches fought for membership, and rifts emerged among the devout. Universities such as Princeton, Brown, and Rutgers were established to train the large number of ministers needed for the increase in religious zeal.

6. C

The British refused the Albany Plan because it would have given the colonies too much freedom, and the colonies rejected it because it didn't give them *enough* independence. However, the failed Albany Plan became a noteworthy springboard for colonial cooperation after 1765.

7. A

After Pontiac's Rebellion in 1762, the British wanted to patch things up with Native American tribes by limiting colonial settlement in the west. The British created the Proclamation of 1763 to defend the colonies from Native American attack and to make peace with the tribes.

8. B

Referring to events like the *Gaspée* incident, the Committees of Correspondence manipulated propaganda to keep the colonists outraged over British discrimination.

9. D

The Enlightenment writings of Locke, Montesquieu, and Rousseau set the tone for colonial rebellion against Great Britain. Locke discussed the necessity for government to guard the natural rights of its citizens. If these natural rights were not protected, the people had the right to overthrow the government and replace it with a better one. The Enlightenment also highlighted reason over religion.

10. A

The delegates of the First Continental Congress conferred about "next steps" or satisfactory types of colonial rebellion against British oppression. Not ready to separate from Britain, the Congress looked for methods to ask for redress of grievances, but it did not seek to start a war or establish an army.

CHAPTER 2

Founding of the Republic to the Civil War: 1783–1877

❯❯ BUILDING A NEW NATION: 1787–1800

The new nation faced high state taxes and debt ratios and challenges from European nations. England kept its troops along the Mississippi River and did not repeal the Navigation Laws. Both England and Spain armed Native Americans along the western frontiers, Spain closed the port of New Orleans to U.S. trade, and France, demanding prompt repayment of war debts, limited U.S. trade in the Caribbean. Without British protection, U.S. merchant ships fell prey to the North African **Barbary pirates**.

Consitutional Convention

In 1787, 12 of the 13 states agreed to send delegates to Philadelphia to improve the Articles of Confederation. On May 25, 1787, 55 delegates from all the states but Rhode Island began meeting secretly. Though George Washington was elected chairperson, **James Madison**, a Virginia delegate,

> ▶ **AP EXPERT TIP**
>
> Highlight key phrases! Your life will be much easier when you need to go back and review text later.

became the convention's leader. Well read in federalism, republicanism, and Lockean theory, he advocated a **central government** whose power exceeded that of the states and believed in the **separation of powers**. The convention chose to scrap the Articles and draft a new document for the nation.

GRANTING LEGISLATIVE AND EXECUTIVE POWER

On May 29 1787, delegates from larger states proposed the **Virginia Plan**, which called for legislative representation based on population. The smaller states countered with the **New Jersey Plan,** which granted equal legislative representation to each state. On June 11, **Roger Sherman** proposed the **Great Compromise (Connecticut Compromise)**, appeasing large states by giving them **proportional representation** in the **lower chamber** (the **House of Representatives**) while granting every state an equal number of seats in the **upper chamber** (the **Senate**). Since it was decided that revenue bills would only go through the (proportionately represented) lower chamber, the larger states *were* given more say in terms of the tax burden all would bear. Concerned about a "**mobocracy**" in which the uneducated would choose an unsuitable president, they set up an **electoral college** whose members would represent their states. Each elector cast two votes—at least one of which had to be for a candidate not from their state—and then all the electors' votes were counted by the President of the Senate.

The Southern states had large populations of slaves and wanted them counted as part of the population, even though they were not considered citizens. If adopted, this policy would have given Southern states greater representation in the House, allowing them to out-vote Northern states on slavery issues. The Northern states agreed to the

"**Three-fifths Compromise**," which counted each slave as three-fifths of a person, and the Southern states accepted that the legal importation of slaves would end in 1808. Northern and Southern delegates compromised, allowing Congress to tax imports but not exports.

RATIFICATION AND ITS AFTERMATH

The Constitution now had to be ratified by at least 9 of the 13 states. Each state held ratification debates between **Federalists** (who supported the Constitution and a strong federal government) and **Anti-Federalists** (who opposed the Constitution and favored strong states' rights). Northern merchants with close ties to British trade networks tended to be Federalists, while people from small Southern farms or western homesteads tended towards Anti-Federalism. Virginians George Washington, James Madison, and John Marshall wooed Anti-Federalists by promising to add a **Bill of Rights**, protecting individual freedoms and state sovereignty. In a series of articles in New York newspapers, Alexander Hamilton, John Jay, and James Madison wrote what would later be republished as **The Federalist Papers**—85 essays urging ratification.

In 1789, soon after the Constitution was adopted, Congress enacted the Bill of Rights. Written mainly by James Madison, these 10 amendments offered protections from abuses by the central government. They were ratified by the states in 1791. The **Judiciary Act of 1789** added many details of court structure to the somewhat vague Judiciary Branch article. It set up a Supreme Court with a presiding chief justice and five associate justices and organized 13 district courts and 3 circuit courts of appeal.

The First President: George Washington, 1789–1797

The Electoral College unanimously elected George Washington as president. He was sworn in on April 30, 1789, in the temporary national capital, New York City. John Adams became vice president. Washington made Thomas Jefferson his secretary of state, Alexander Hamilton his secretary of the treasury, Henry Knox his secretary of war, and (once the Judiciary Act was passed) Edmund Randolph the attorney general. President Washington referred to these four officials as his "**cabinet**" and conferred with them regularly, a practice that goes on to this day.

ECONOMIC POLICY

In 1790, Secretary of the Treasury Hamilton issued a **Report on Public Credit** in which he advocated paying off domestic debt by selling bonds, which would raise money while encouraging bondholders to invest in the future of the United States. His **Report on Manufactures** (1791) called for industrialization and strong protective tariffs to safeguard domestic industry. His five-part financial plan called for boosting national credit by **funding at par**—paying all debts at face value plus interest, and he wanted the federal government to take on all state debts. He wanted to create revenue through taxes on imported goods and wanted to found a stable national bank.

In regards to government acquisition of state debt, Northern states with large war debts were thrilled, but Southern states were not. As a compromise Hamilton accepted Jefferson's request for a permanent national capital situated on the banks of the Potomac River between Maryland and Virginia. He also tried to augment income gained from the relatively low (8 percent) tariff on imports established by the **Revenue Act of 1789** by imposing excise taxes on whiskey. However, backwoods Pennsylvania farmers who distilled and sold whiskey protested the new tax with such force that President Washington had to send a militia to stop their **Whiskey Rebellion**. Washington's action demonstrated the power of the new national government to enforce its laws.

Though the **Bank of the United States (BUS)** was ultimately established in 1791, the wisdom of doing so was highly contested. To be principally owned by the federal government, the bank would guard national treasury funds. A **strict constructionist** who believed in interpreting the Constitution strictly as written, Thomas Jefferson thought that the

Constitution did not allow for a national bank. **Loose constructionists**, including Hamilton himself, believed that the Constitution's **"elastic" clause** granted Congress "implied powers" since there was a need to collect and keep federal money.

THE PARTY SYSTEM

Hamilton and other Federalists held fast to then-conservative ideology and believed that Federal power should stand above state power. Championing states' rights, the then-liberal Anti-Federalists evolved into the **Democratic-Republicans** supported by Thomas Jefferson.

Foreign and Domestic Issues

FOREIGN POLICY

As the **French Revolution** (1789–1799) became a world war involving Britain and the Caribbean, America was challenged. Jefferson felt that the United States should remain France's ally, while Hamilton, who wanted to maintain trade with all nations, called for U.S. neutrality. With his **Neutrality Proclamation of 1793**, President Washington sided with Hamilton. However, England began seizing American ships on the Atlantic, taking cargo and impressing their crews into military service, until the president sent **John Jay**, the chief justice of the Supreme Court, to negotiate with the British. While **Jay's Treaty** did not stop British ships from seizing American vessels, it did call for the removal of British forts in the American West, establish a means to define the border with Canada, allow for trade in the British West Indies, and determine a way to compensate Americans for their losses at sea. Washington sent Thomas Pinckney to negotiate boundaries, the right to navigate the Mississippi River, and right of deposit at the Port of New Orleans with Spain. **Pinckney's Treaty** was ratified in 1796.

DOMESTIC ISSUES

The new nation had to deal with the constant threat of Native American attack. Tribes who had been armed by the British rose up against American settlers pushing westwards. In 1794, U.S. soldiers fought and decisively triumphed over Native American fighters in Ohio. As a result, in the **Treaty of Greenville of 1795**, those tribes surrendered their claims to land in Ohio and Indiana and then had to move west from their homes, putting them into almost continual battle with other tribes.

President John Adams, 1797–1801

In 1797, **John Adams** took office as the second president of the United States. George Washington delivered a **Farewell Address** in which he asked the nation to remain neutral in European affairs and refrain from forming "factions" (political parties). Thomas Jefferson became Adams's vice president.

FOREIGN AFFAIRS

President Adams sent a delegation to Paris to negotiate an agreement that would stop France's seizures of American ships. Arriving in France, the delegation was approached by three French agents, named only as X, Y, and Z, who demanded that the Americans both lend them a large sum of money and pay them to speak to French officials. The delegation refused to comply and called this the **XYZ Affair.** As Federalists called for immediate military action, an undeclared naval war with France ensued. From 1798 to 1800, this "quasi-war" went on, principally in the West Indies. To avoid total war, Adams sent envoys to meet with **Napoleon** and his foreign minister **Talleyrand**. As an outcome of this meeting, which was known as the **Convention of 1800**, the Franco-American Alliance was terminated, the United States agreed to pay for damages inflicted on French vessels, and all-out war was avoided.

DOMESTIC AFFAIRS

After the congressional elections of 1798, tension between the Federalists and Democratic-Republicans intensified. The Federalists began enacting laws aimed at silencing the opposition. The **Alien Acts** increased the residency required for citizenship from 5 to 14 years and gave the president power to detain and/or deport enemy aliens in times of war. The **Sedition Act,** written to silence Democratic-Republicans, made it illegal to criticize the president or Congress and imposed a fine or imprisonment upon violators (such as newspaper editors). Angered by this violation of the right to free speech guaranteed by the First Amendment, Democratic-Republicans urged states to pass statutes to **nullify** these acts. Thomas Jefferson in the **Kentucky Resolutions** and James Madison in the **Virginia Resolutions** argued that because the Constitution was formed by a compact of states, the states themselves could decide if a law was unconstitutional, and if so ignore it. This "**compact theory**" of government would be used during the nullification crisis of 1832.

The Federalists lost much of the momentum they had gained in 1798 before the election of 1800. Although Thomas Jefferson defeated John Adams in the popular vote, he tied with Aaron Burr in the electoral college, leaving the decision to the House of Representatives. The Federalists, who still controlled the House, debated for four days. Eventually, the House chose Thomas Jefferson as president.

❯ JEFFERSONIAN AMERICA: 1800–1816

The Louisiana Purchase

The **Louisiana Territory** belonged to Spain when Napoleon of France purchased it secretly in 1800. Jefferson sent ministers to negotiate with Napoleon in Paris, instructing them to offer $10 million for New Orleans and a strip of land that extended to Florida. To their surprise, Napoleon offered them the entire Louisiana territory for $15 million. Though the Constitution gave no power to the president to authorize such a purchase, Jefferson swayed from his strict-constructionist views and went ahead. Hoping to form an agricultural empire with access to a route by water from the Missouri River to the Pacific Ocean, Jefferson sent a team led by **Meriwether Lewis** and **William Clark** to explore. Starting out from St. Louis, Missouri in 1804, they traveled all the way to the Oregon Coast and returned in 1806.

The Marshall Court

The Federalists passed the **Judiciary Act of 1801**, which created 16 new judgeships just in time for President Adams to appoint them on the eve of his departure from office (hence the term "**midnight judges**"). To prevent these men from assuming these lifetime appointments, Jefferson ordered his secretary of state, **James Madison**, not to deliver the commissions. **William Marbury**, one of the judges blocked from office, sued under the **Judiciary Act of 1789**, which gave the Supreme Court the authority to enforce judicial commissions. Chief Justice **John Marshall**, a staunch Federalist, avoided the issue of issuing or not issuing a **writ of mandamus** (an order forcing the administration to deliver the commissions). Instead, he ruled that the Constitution did not authorize the Supreme Court to issue such writs, and since the Constitution is the supreme law of the land, the Court and the Jefferson administration must adhere to it. With this decision, Marshall established the Court's power of judicial review—that is, interpreting whether or not a law is Constitutional.

Jefferson tried **impeachment** of Federalist judges. While the House voted to impeach Supreme Court Justice Samuel Chase because of his partisan views, the Senate, finding no evidence of "high crimes and misdemeanors," refused to convict him, thus upholding the separation of powers between legislature and the judiciary.

Jefferson's Second Term

Though he easily won reelection in 1804, Jefferson was beset by political issues. In 1804, states ratified the **Twelfth Amendment** to the Constitution, which ended the previous custom of giving the vice presidency to the runner-up in a presidential election. **Aaron Burr**, who had been vice president during Jefferson's first term, was not selected as Jefferson's running mate for the later election. Instead, he ran for governor of New York and lost, and accused Alexander Hamilton of defaming him. Then, later in 1804, Burr challenged Hamilton to a duel, during which he shot and fatally wounded Hamilton. Burr was involved in a secession plot in 1806. Known as the **Burr Conspiracy,** it involved getting control of Spanish Mexico and joining it to the Louisiana territory to form a new country to the west. When President Jefferson heard of this, he had Burr arrested and tried for treason, but the prosecution could produce no credible witnesses and Burr was acquitted and freed.

Jefferson's cousin, John Randolph, angry that Jefferson had moderated his strong states' rights position, led the **Quids**, a small, radical group of Republicans who accused Jefferson of being involved in a faulty land deal in the Yazoo region of Georgia. Jefferson agreed to pay restitution to the land companies, which Randolph and the Quids portrayed as bribery. The **Yazoo land controversy** created a schism within the Republican Party that would plague Jefferson for the rest of his term.

The North African Barbary pirates continued to seize American merchant ships in the Mediterranean. Presidents Washington and Adams had paid protection money to the North African nations, and now Tripoli was demanding even more money. Jefferson refused to pay and sent the navy to stop the pirates. These **Tripolitan Wars** (1801 to 1805) put a damper on the pirates and earned the United States respect from overseas. However, the **Napoleonic War** raging in Europe created larger problems. With his **Berlin Decree** of 1806, Napoleon attempted to cut Britain off from the rest of the world, which included blocking neutral American merchant ships. England retaliated with **Orders in Council** by closing all ports under French control and confiscating ships—including American vessels—that did not stop in England. Napoleon then issued his **Milan Decree** of 1807, in which ships stopping in Britain would be seized. In response to these measures, Jefferson signed the **Embargo Act of 1807**, which prevented all American ships from leaving U.S. ports.

The Madison Presidency, 1809–1817

Republican **James Madison** won the 1808 election. The one-year **Non-Intercourse Act of 1809** replaced the Embargo Act and allowed trade with all foreign nations except England and France. Congress then passed **Macon's Bill Number 2**, which sought to lift trade restrictions against England and France when they honored U.S. neutrality. France did so, in words but not actions, and England continued to harass American ships. **War hawks**, such as **Henry Clay** and **John C. Calhoun**, wanted to stop the British from arming Native Americans against settlers at the frontiers. **The Battle of Tippecanoe,** in present-day Indiana, occurred after a surprise attack on settlers (led by **Shawnee** brothers **Tecumseh** and the **Prophet**) was repelled by **General William Henry Harrison's** men, who then burned the tribal settlement of Tippecanoe, removing the Native American threat in the west.

The War of 1812

Already infuriated by British seizure of American ships and impressment of American sailors, American war hawks now pushed for the conquest of Canada. In June 1812, their pressure in the face of continuing British trade restrictions caused President Madison to ask for (and be granted) a declaration of war at the same time that the trade restrictions were being repealed in England. This "Second War of Independence" was small and disappointing for the United States, whose devastated economy and inadequate military were hard pressed by the conflict. In August 1814, the English burned Washington, D.C., to the ground. When American soldiers successfully held Fort McHenry (near Baltimore, Maryland), Francis Scott Key captured the moment in the song "**The Star Spangled Banner.**"

In what was essentially a split between the Federalist East Coast and the rest of the nation, the New England states were vehemently opposed to the war and Republican policy in general. Meeting in Connecticut, Federalist delegates to the **Hartford Convention** (December 1814–January 1815) considered amendments to the Constitution and even secession from the Union. However, they arrived in Washington to make their demands just as news of the Treaty of Ghent and Andrew Jackson's victory at New Orleans swept in. This heralded the demise of the Federalist Party, which was routed by James Monroe in 1816's elections.

The Treaty of Ghent (December 24, 1814), which officially ended the war, was signed in Belgium. It returned conquered territories to their rightful owners, restoring the U.S./Canada border to its prewar boundaries. The United States had become more independent from European markets, marking the start of America's Industrial Revolution. Ironically, America's most impressive victory (at the **Battle of New Orleans**), which occurred when General Andrew Jackson and his Southern troops defeated the British army and ended its push to control the Mississippi River, was fought two weeks after the treaty ending the war had been signed.

❯ THE NATIONAL SPIRIT AND MARKET REVOLUTION: 1817–1850

The Monroe Presidency, 1817–1825

Heralded as **"The Era of Good Feeling,"** the times were not really harmonious, as tension regarding tariffs, slavery, and power within the Republican Party grew. Monroe persuaded Congress to enact the **Tariff of 1816**, America's first **"protective tariff,"** a 20 percent duty on all imported goods to protect American industry.

This precipitated a sectional crisis. Three men became principal spokespeople for their **constituencies**. Secretary of State **John Calhoun**, a South Carolinian, first supported the tariff, believing the South's future lay in developing a manufacturing base, but later opposed it because he felt it enriched northern merchants at the expense of southern farmers and plantation owners. New Englander **Daniel Webster** called for conditions aiding his region's unrestricted development. **Henry Clay** of Kentucky believed that the tariff would help the South to establish manufacturing and bring in revenue. Clay promoted his **American System** of internal improvements, which called for tariffs, renewing the Bank of the United States, and building up **infrastructure** (turnpikes, roads, canals).

The Panic of 1819

The Second Bank of the United States (BUS) caused a financial crisis by **overspeculating** on land in the west. It then attempted to control the **inflation** the war had produced by pulling back on credit to state banks during the recession that followed the war and demanding payment in **specie** (coins). Many western **"wildcat banks,"** which had made many loans to frontierspeople, did not have enough on hand to pay BUS. BUS subsequently forced these banks to foreclose on farmers who could not immediately pay back their debts, which made many people landless. The state of Maryland fought BUS by passing a bill requiring all banks not chartered by the state legislature to pay a tax. In 1819, the Supreme Court nullified the law in **McCullough v. Maryland**, a landmark decision dictating that state laws cannot hinder Constitutional measures passed by the Federal government.

The Missouri Compromise

In 1819, the country consisted of 22 states, of which half were slave holding and half were free. As Missouri, vying for statehood, threatened to tip the balance to the South, New York proposed the **Tallmadge Amendment** (which would allow bringing no more slaves into Missouri and emancipating the children of slaves there at age 25). Southerners crushed the amendment but tempers were flaring. Then **"the Great Compromiser," Henry Clay**, proposed the

Missouri Compromise of 1820. Under the bill, Missouri's entrance into the union as a slave state would be balanced by the admission of Maine as a free state, and slavery would not be permitted in future states admitted above the **36° 30'** line. The compromise was accepted and held for 34 years.

President Monroe's **1823** address to Congress (written by **John Quincy Adams**) warned Europe to stay out of the Western Hemisphere and called for "nonintervention" in Latin America—this address is known as **the Monroe Doctrine**.

Intense Economic and Social Changes

Between 1820 and 1860, as the population increased dramatically and roads, canals, steamboats, and railroads sprang up, a national market economy took hold in the United States. The west was growing the nation's grain, the east was holding the industrial reins, and the southern plantation economy (bolstered by the use of the **cotton gin**) continued to grow. The population continued to double every 25 years, and was further increased by an influx of the Irish (fleeing the Irish potato famine) and Germans (seeking refuge from political/economic hardship). The immigrant tide was met by an Anglo-American (**nativist**) backlash. These nativists, who opposed immigration and wanted to deny political office to Roman Catholics, formed a political party called the **American Party**. It was also called the **Know-Nothing Party** because its members, who met in secret, refused to say what they stood for, answering, "I know nothing."

❯❯ JACKSON'S DEMOCRACY: 1824–1837

The Rise of the Party System

As an increasing number of middle- and lower-class men became involved in the political process, "**the rise of the common man**" heralded a more democratic society. By 1820, many states had adopted universal male suffrage, which did not limit voting only to those who owned property. New third parties arose, and in the election of 1824, amidst much mudslinging, four Republicans vied for the presidency. Though Andrew Jackson won the most popular votes, no candidate had an electoral vote majority, so the House had to choose the president. Candidate Henry Clay threw his support to John Quincy Adams, resulting in Adams's election by the House.

John Quincy Adams, 1825–1829

President Adams appointed Henry Clay as secretary of state, thereby marring his presidency with the taint of the implied **corrupt bargain** since Clay, as speaker of the House, had campaigned for him. In his inaugural address, Adams proposed building highways and canals, creating a national university, and advancing science by underwriting experiments, but his quiet presidency accomplished few of those things.

Challenges to Federal Authority

Still on the bench of the Supreme Court and still upholding his Federalist beliefs, Chief Justice John Marshall continued to rule for federal power over state power. In another ruling, *Gibbons v. Ogden* (1824), his court upheld federal control of interstate commerce. At issue was whether Congress could supersede a New York state law that had granted a steamship company sole travel rights in New York waters. Invoking the commerce clause, Marshall ruled that the state-sanctioned monopoly was unconstitutional, and Congress trumped states even when commerce fell within state borders.

New England merchants and manufacturers wanted high protective tariffs, which would induce Americans to buy American goods. The South, which relied on trade with Europe, did not want to antagonize European nations. **The Tariff of 1828,** backed by New England, had been blasted as the **"Tariff of Abominations."** John C. Calhoun contended that trade was essential to Southern farmers, the tariff was unconstitutional, and Southern states should nullify it.

Andrew Jackson, 1929–1937

Jackson ran as a Democrat against Henry Clay, who was a **National Republican** (a party formed specifically to oppose Jackson, whose members would be called **Whigs** after 1836).

The Charter of the Bank of the United States was due to expire in 1832. Jackson, who did not believe that the government should involve itself in economic affairs, vetoed the bill to recharter the bank and then killed the BUS by removing all federal funds it held and transferring them to various state banks (**"pet banks"**). As prices in the country soared ruinously, Jackson issued the **Specie Circular**, which required buyers of federal land to pay in hard coins ("specie") rather than banknotes, thereby causing paper money to plummet in value. This brought about the **Panic of 1837** and left the United States without a federal bank repository until the Civil War.

PROBLEMS REGARDING TARIFFS

The Tariff of 1828 prompted the Daniel Webster/Robert Hayne debate on the Senate floor in 1830, in which Webster made Hayne's calls for Southern nullification and succession (the **"Nullification Crisis"**) seem treasonous. However, in an attempt to placate the infuriated South, Jackson supported the **Tariff of 1832,** which brought the 45 percent tariff down to 35 percent. The South threatened to secede if Jackson tried to collect the duties by force. Jackson asked Congress for the 1833 **Force Bill,** which gave the president the power to have the military collect tariffs, if necessary. As the possibility of civil war grew, Henry Clay proposed a tariff, enacted in 1833, that slowly reduced the tariff percentage—a compromise.

In the interest of upholding states' rights (without imperiling the Union), Jackson vetoed more bills than his six predecessors combined. While increasing the power of the presidency, he sought to expand democracy. A proponent of the **spoils system**, Jackson appointed his supporters to government positions. He also believed in rotating officials to keep appointees on their toes. Critics lamented that many friends he appointed to his unofficial "**kitchen**" **cabinet** did not have to answer to Congress.

JACKSON VERSUS NATIVE AMERICANS

Jackson signed the **Indian Removal Act** into law in 1830; by 1835, it had forcibly removed some 100,000 "civilized" Cherokee, Chickasaw, Choctaw, Creek, and Seminole Indians from their homes in Mississippi, Alabama, Florida, Georgia, and what is now Illinois. The Cherokees took their case to the Supreme Court, which, in *Cherokee Nation v. Georgia* (1831), ruled that the tribe had no right to sue for jurisdiction over its homelands. However, when the Marshall court ruled in favor of the Cherokees in *Worcester v. Georgia* (1832), President Jackson did not come to the Cherokees' aid, and 4,000 Cherokees died on the **Trail of Tears**, the march from Georgia to Oklahoma.

❱ SECTIONAL TENSION GROWS: 1820–1850

The Industrial North and Agricultural Northwest

Spurred by the growth of transportation, the northern United States experienced industrial growth. Textile factories dominated and brought rapid population growth to cities, followed by overcrowding, disease, and rising crime. The Old

Northwest (Ohio, Indiana, Illinois, Michigan, Wisconsin, and Minnesota) was closely linked to the industrial North by rail lines and canals, and regionally specialized in growing corn and wheat. As grain shipments to the northern cities of New York, Boston, and Philadelphia increased, the river and port cities of St. Louis, Cleveland, and Chicago grew, too.

The Agrarian South

The plantation/cash crop economy of the South had been in existence ever since **Eli Whitney** in 1793 had invented the **cotton gin**, a device that separated cotton fibers from seeds, a painstaking job previously done by hand. As the market grew, the demand for slave labor grew with it, causing a fourfold increase in the **peculiar institution** (slavery) over 50 years. Many laws and codes were passed to protect slaveholders from losses connected with their most expensive and risky investments: their slaves. Slaves were property, and any hint of rebellion was punished. Though educating a slave was forbidden, many of them were taught to read and write. By 1860, the South had 250,000 free blacks or people of mixed race (**mulattos**). The **planter aristocracy** (with at least 100 slaves and 1,000 farmable acres) topped the social ladder.

The Western Frontier

Those who chose to venture out and settle the lands beyond the Mississippi River knew little except that the way was dangerous and the Native Americans, who had been driven out of their lands and into the Great Plains, would not make life easy for white settlers. Many settlers lived in huts and cabins along lakes, rivers, and streams, struggling to establish farms.

❯ ANTEBELLUM RENAISSANCE: 1790–1860

Religious Revivalism

With its roots in the Calvinist fervor of the 1790s, which grew up in response to the liberal doctrine of leaders like Jefferson, the **Second Great Awakening** gained momentum when revivalist preachers toured the United States in the early 19th century. Spearheaded by Presbyterian minister **Charles G. Finney,** the movement played on emotions and instilled the fear of damnation in thousands. Soon, Methodists and Baptists joined in, sending clergy out across the south and west, preaching at tent revivals, "saving" large numbers of people, and, in the process, becoming the two largest denominations in the country. The new converts, who were mostly middle-class people, then began a social reform movement that would reach all the way into the 1860s. Their idea was that **perfectionism** (attaining a level that resembled that of Jesus) could be attained through faith, hard work, education, and temperance.

THE TEMPERANCE MOVEMENT

With the aim of encouraging drinkers to limit their intake of alcohol, the **American Temperance Society**, whose members were mainly middle-class women, led a movement that targeted German and Irish populations as well as Anglo-Americans. The **Maine Law** of 1851 prohibited the use and sale of alcohol in Maine and inspired similar legislation in 12 other states.

MENTAL & PHYSICAL HEALTH

Dorothea Dix spearheaded the movement to improve the conditions (in mental asylums and jails) of those who were mentally ill and to change the nation's penal system from one that punished offenders to one that reformed them. Working with the idea that criminal tendencies developed in childhood, **Horace Mann** led the movement to reform the U.S. public school system by making attendance compulsory and free (funded by the states).

THE ABOLITION MOVEMENT

Gaining ground in the Second Great Awakening, **abolitionist** belief held that slavery was sinful and had to be eliminated. In 1831, a newspaper espousing the ending of slavery (*The Liberator*) was formed by **William Lloyd Garrison**, who went on to found the **American Antislavery Society** in 1833. Garrison's radicalism (he derided the Constitution as being a pro-slavery document) alienated the society's moderates, and the movement broke into two parts: the **Liberty Party**, which accepted women as members, and the **Foreign Antislavery Society**, which did not. The movement also embraced free blacks, whose leaders included **Harriet Tubman**, **Sojourner Truth**, and **Frederick Douglass**. Douglass published an antislavery journal called *The North Star.* Tubman and Truth were also among many individuals who ran an elaborate network called the **Underground Railroad** that helped their runaway brethren escape. Violent slave uprisings, such as **Nat Turner's Rebellion** in Virginia in 1831, did happen, but Turner's Rebellion brought only the deaths of over 50 whites followed by the retaliatory slaying of hundreds of slaves.

Women's Rights versus The Cult of Domesticity

As advances in transportation and technology changed ways of life, taking women from the fields and into **women's work** (which meant tending home and children) and removing the economic need to produce many children to pitch in as farmhands, middle-class white birthrates dropped. The **cult of domesticity,** which confined women to their housekeeping roles, prevailed. Even within the abolitionist movement, women had second-class status. In 1838, **Sarah and Angelina Grimke** spoke up against male dominance and the "cult" of male superiority, foreshadowing a meeting of **feminists**, including **Lucretia Mott**, **Elizabeth Cady Stanton**, and **Susan B. Anthony**, at **Seneca Falls, New York.** There the **Declaration of Sentiments**, which called for universal suffrage that included women, was written.

Utopian Societies

The **Church of Jesus Christ of Latter Day Saints** (the **Mormons**) was formally organized by **Joseph Smith** in 1830, following his 1823 conversion experience during which he said he was visited by the angel **Moroni**, who revealed the location of a set of golden plates containing sacred text. Persecuted at home in New York, the Mormons headed west. In Illinois, where Smith was murdered by a mob, **Brigham Young** assumed leadership and took his people on to settle in **Deseret** (now called Utah). Because Mormons practiced **polygamy**, their territory of Utah was not granted statehood until the church agreed to ban men from taking multiple wives.

Transcendentalists

This group emphasized the connection between man and nature, spurned materialism, and embraced self-reliance. Writers such as **Ralph Waldo Emerson** and **Henry David Thoreau** spoke for the movement in their works. Thoreau's *Walden* chronicled his experiment in isolated living in the Massachusetts woods near Walden Pond. In 1841, a group of transcendentalists formed a communal settlement called **Brook Farm**, which lasted until 1849, when it had to close because of debt.

The Emergence of an American Culture

In the visual arts, portraits, historical scenes, and still lifes gave way to large-scale, romantic landscapes. Thomas Cole and Fredrick Church of the **Hudson River School** of painting honored the impressive American terrain. The nationalistic spirit that prevailed after 1812 fueled the nation's authors through the 1850s. New York's **Knickerbocker** writers, such as Washington Irving, created an American fictional tradition that drew on domestic settings and characters, while **James Fenimore Cooper** glorified Western life and writers such as **Nathaniel Hawthorne** and **Herman Melville** grappled with the religious issues that occupied the nation.

❯❯ MANIFEST DESTINY: 1830–1860

Popularized by a journalist in 1845, the phrase **manifest destiny,** with its assumption that God had granted all the land between the great oceans to the United States, became emblematic of westward expansion. By 1840, thousands were settling the region that would become Texas; by 1943, thousands more were traversing the dangerous **Oregon Trail**. Families traveled the route in caravans of 10 to 20 covered wagons, advancing no more than 15 miles a day on a journey that would last for 6 months. The journey transformed the lives of women accustomed to the traditional mother/homemaker role.

Settlers and Sioux Indians pushing westward to hunt buffalo began to displace the Native Americans who had lived in the Great Plains for centuries. The Sioux, who used guns and horses to advantage, had been advancing westward to hunt buffalo and fight for territory since the mid-1700s, and in the early 1800s, the Sioux had control over much of the Great Plains.

The Martin Van Buren Presidency, 1837–1841

Van Buren's presidency was burdened with the consequences of Jackson's policies: the Panic of 1837 and the economic depression that followed. He was powerless to revive the economy, and because he maintained much of Jackson's platform he remained unpopular through his term. When Van Buren ran a second time, he was vigorously opposed by the Whigs, who advertised their slate with the slogan **"Tippecanoe and Tyler, too."** (Presidential candidate William Henry Harrison was a hero of the Battle of Tippecanoe, and John Tyler was his running mate.) The Whigs carried the election. Four weeks after taking office, Harrison died and Tyler took office.

Problems in the Territories

In 1838, frontiersmen clashed, rhetoric heated up, and troops marched to the U.S./Canadian border. Fortunately, war was averted when the United States and England negotiated a treaty (the **Webster-Ashburton Treaty, 1842**), that divided up the contested Canadian (English-owned) territory and settled the northern boundary of Minnesota.

THE ONGOING QUESTION OF TEXAS

In 1821, when Texas belonged to newly independent Mexico, Mexico sought farmers from the United States. By the 1830s, when these settlers and their slaves outnumbered Mexicans, slavery was banned in Texas. In addition, Mexico demanded that all residents become Catholic. After the Texans refused to follow these rules and **Antonio Lopez de Santa Anna**, Mexico's military dictator, cracked down on them, the Texans revolted. In 1836, led by **Sam Houston**, they declared Texas an independent republic. Santa Anna's forces then attacked the **Alamo** and killed everyone there, after which Houston's forces routed and captured Santa Anna at the San Jacinto River, forcing him to grant the Republic of Texas (**the Lone Star Republic**) independence. At the very end of his administration, Tyler saw President James K. Polk's victory as a mandate for expansionism, and Texas joined the Union in 1844.

James K. Polk, 1845–1849

In the election of 1844, James K. Polk of Tennessee defeated Henry Clay, largely because of Polk's strongly expansionist views. Enraged at the United States for annexing Texas, Mexico demanded the territory's return. Polk then sent his envoy, John Slidell, to Mexico's capitol to declare that the United States would honor Texas's original Nueces River boundary and to ask to purchase California. He also sent the U.S. Army under Zachary Taylor to the disputed southern border of Texas in January of 1846. In April, a Mexican force crossed the **Rio Grande** and attacked Taylor's men, killing several, prompting Congress to declare war on Mexico. The **Wilmot Proviso**, which specified that slavery would not be permitted in the new land acquired from the war with Mexico, was attached to a bill making its way through Congress. That the bill passed in the House but failed in the Senate signaled a new stage of crisis pitting North against South over issues of slavery, states' rights, and representation. The United States won quick, decisive military victories in California and Texas, effectively ending the Mexican-American War by September of 1847. Under rabblerousing Major John Fremont, California had been declared the independent **Bear Flag Republic**. The **Treaty of Guadalupe Hidalgo**, signed in February 1848, granted the United States California and most of the Southwest (today's New Mexico, Arizona, Utah, Nevada), while the United States agreed to pay $15 million in reparations to Mexico.

❯❯ ON THE BRINK OF CIVIL WAR: 1848–1860

A Three-Party Election

The 1848 election pitted Democrat Lewis Cass, a proponent of **popular sovereignty** (each territory's citizens would vote on whether to permit slavery), against Whig candidate Zachary Taylor and Martin Van Buren, now allied with the antislavery **Free-Soil** party.

Zachary Taylor's Brief Presidency, 1849–1850

In 1848, gold had been discovered in the west. As a hoard of **49ers** surged out to seek their fortunes, California drafted a new constitution forbidding slavery and sought statehood. Henry Clay came up with a **compromise** to admit California as a free state, admit New Mexico and Utah while letting them decide their status, ban slave trade in Washington, D.C., enact a stricter **Fugitive Slave Law**, and compensate Texas for forgoing claims to part of New Mexico. Taylor died suddenly on a hot day in July 1850, probably of gastroenteritis, though conspiracy theorists believe he may have been poisoned.

Millard Fillmore's Presidency, 1850–1853

The Compromise of 1850 bought time for the Union. With California in as a free state, the North gained the political upper hand, but the strict Fugitive Slave Law (which re-enslaved those who had made it to freedom, denied legal rights to captured blacks, and punished anyone helping an escaped slave) was problematic. The Underground Railroad increased operations and **Harriet Beecher Stowe** wrote *Uncle Tom's Cabin*.

President Franklin Pierce, 1853–1857

A New Hampshirite with Southern sympathies, Pierce's greatest presidential achievement was buying land from Mexico (the 1854 **Gadsden Purchase** of parts of present-day Arizona and New Mexico) for a southern transcontinental railroad route. Meanwhile, the slavery debate raged, as **abolitionists** listed the evils of slavery while **apologists** justified it. **George Fitzhugh**, an apologist leader, argued that since slaves were provided for by their owners, they were much better off than Northern "wage slaves."

The Kansas Nebraska Act of 1854

This act was designed to divide the Nebraska Territory into Kansas and Nebraska. Each area's citizens would determine their region's stand on slavery (with Kansas presumably becoming a free state and Nebraska a slave state). The two factions began to fight, earning the region the name **Bleeding Kansas**. The pro-slavery faction organized a government and drafted a constitution that protected existing slaveholders, whether or not the populace voted for no slavery. The state's anti-slavers revolted and formed their own legislature, and violence escalated. In 1856, armed border ruffians viciously attacked the Free-Soil town of Lawrence. A band of abolitionists led by **John Brown** retaliated, attacking farms in the area with equal savagery. Disaffected people banded together to form a new party. This **Republican Party** opposed the expansion of slavery and the Kansas-Nebraska Act. Though the Republicans did not win the presidency, they gained momentum among free states.

President James Buchanan, 1857–1861

President Buchanan, another "doughface," or Northerner with Southern sympathies, hoped to quell sectional differences to no avail. ***Dred Scott v. Sanford*** involved Dred Scott, a slave who had been moved from Missouri to Wisconsin and Illinois for five years before returning to Missouri. Supported by abolitionists, Scott sued his master, claiming that the years spent in free territory had made him a free man, a status he should keep even after his return to a slave state. Taney's ruling declared that African Americans had no citizenship protections under the Constitution and that Congress could not deny individuals their property under the U.S. Constitution. Slaves were property; therefore, the **Missouri Compromise of 1820**, which stripped slaveholders of their human property when they moved north past a particular boundary line, was unconstitutional. The decision widened the rift between North and South. Hoping to arm slaves, overthrow the whites, and create a black free state, abolitionist John Brown and his band staged a raid on the federal arsenal at **Harper's Ferry, Virginia, in 1859**. They held the arsenal for two days before being captured and subsequently hanged. Brown was hailed as a martyr in the North and derided in the South.

The Rise of Lincoln and the Election of 1860

In 1858, a little-known Republican country lawyer named **Abraham Lincoln** ran for the Senate in Illinois. Though he lost to Senator Stephen A. Douglas, their debates about slavery—Lincoln warned of pervasive "Slave Power," and Douglas advocated each territory deciding the issue by popular sovereignty—gave Lincoln a national reputation. By 1960, as nominating conventions began, the Union was on the verge of breaking apart. The Republican Party made Lincoln their candidate and adopted a platform (nonextension of slavery into the territories, a protective tariff, rights for immigrants, a transcontinental railroad, federally financed infrastructure in the west, free homesteads for citizens on publicly held land) that could appeal to a broad range of voters. The Southern Democrats promised to secede from the Union if Lincoln was elected. Under this threat, the **Constitutional Union Party** was formed by Whigs, Know-Nothings, and moderates who hoped to get enough Southern support to hold the Union together by preventing a Lincoln victory. Lincoln got about 40 percent of the popular vote, but by carrying states with large numbers of electoral votes, he won the presidency with 180 electoral votes. Four days after election results came in, South Carolina voted to secede from the Union, to be joined by six more Southern states within the next six weeks. In February of 1861, a Southern nation, the **Confederate States of America**, was formed with **Jefferson Davis** as president.

❯ THE CIVIL WAR: 1861–1865

Northern Realities

Industrially and financially strong, the North controlled the nation's banks, railroads, and factories and could block Southern trade with the rest of the world. However, it needed many men and munitions and the ability to transport them over long distances and would have to levy an income tax (the first one ever), raise excise taxes, and issue **greenbacks** to replace gold as the wartime currency. Starting with a volunteer army, the Union could not maintain forces of sufficient size and had to enact the first federal **conscription** law in 1863. In the **New York Draft Riots**, sparked by angry Irish-Americans who were willing to fight to preserve the union but not for emancipation, 500 people died and whole city blocks were burned.

Southern Realities

The South needed only to defend its territories and so required fewer overall troops than the North. However, with its agrarian economy, the South was at a disadvantage when it came to gathering the basic resources needed to wage an effective war. Also, if cut off from railway links to the West, it would have limited means to transport men, goods, or supplies. The Southern economy would also suffer when Europe cut back its cotton purchases once the civil war was underway. Though relying on volunteers at the start, the South had problems replenishing the ranks. The wealthy classes found ways to avoid service, Appalachian hillbillies refused to join the army, and the Confederacy feared to arm slaves for service lest they turn against their masters. The Confederacy had to enact conscription in 1862.

The Battles of the War

The First Battle of Bull Run occurred near **Manassas**, Virginia, in July 1861, where Confederate (**gray**) forces led by **General "Stonewall" Jackson** drove the Union (**blue**) troops out. With **General Winfield Scott** in command, the North drew up a four-phase plan, the **Anaconda Plan**, meant to wear down the Confederacy. In Phase One, the Union Navy would cut the South off from supplies and trade by blockading all its ports of entry. In Phase Two, the Union would take control of the Mississippi River, thereby cutting the Confederacy in half. Phase Three would march the Union army through the heart of the South. Phase Four would complete victory by capturing **Richmond, Virginia**, the Confederate capital.

THE SECOND BATTLE OF BULL RUN

After Union General McClellan's troops were routed from Virginia's peninsula region by Confederate General **Robert E. Lee** in March 1862, and General John Pope was put in command of the Union army, General Lee took advantage of the lull to engage Union troops again at Manassas in August (Second Battle of Bull Run), forcing the Pope army to retreat.

THE BATTLE OF ANTIETAM, SEPTEMBER 1862

Lee led his men into Union Maryland, where McClellan cut off Lee's army at Antietam Creek. In this bloodiest day of the war, more than 23,000 men were lost or wounded. Lee retreated to Virginia, but McClellan did not pursue him, which so enraged Lincoln that he replaced him with **General Ambrose Burnside.** Antietam was a deciding battle because it deterred Europe from aiding the South while giving Lincoln the victory he wanted in order to issue a preliminary Emancipation Proclamation, which he did right after the battle.

THE BATTLE OF FREDERICKSBURGH, DECEMBER 1862

After General Burnside's aggressive stance did not win this battle, he was replaced by **General Joseph Hooker.**

THE NAVAL WAR

In 1862, the first **ironclad ships** revolutionized naval warfare. The South launched the **CSS *Merrimac*.** However, the Union sent its own ironclad ship, the **USS *Monitor*,** to combat the *Merrimac*. Their five-hour skirmish in March ended in a draw and launched a new chapter in naval history.

CONTROL OF THE MISSISSIPPI

As he cut his way through Kentucky and Tennessee, Union **General Ulysses S. Grant** won the bloody **Battle of Shiloh** in April of 1862. A year later, he had control of the port city of New Orleans and almost all the Mississippi River region. After taking the fortified city of Vicksburg, Mississippi, after a seven-week siege, the Union controlled the entire Mississippi River and surrounding regions.

THE BATTLE OF GETTYSBURG

Though the Confederates successfully flanked Union forces to win the battle at **Chancellorsville**, Virginia, they lost 13,000 men, including their general, who was killed by friendly fire. In a final effort to invade the North, attract foreign supporters, and force the Union to sue for peace, General Lee invaded Pennsylvania. The Union army met him at **Gettysburg,** in southern Pennsylvania, for the deadliest and most important battle of the war. After three days of fighting, 53,000 men had been killed and wounded, and Lee was forced to retreat to Virginia.

SHERMAN'S CONTRIBUTIONS

Chosen by General Grant to lead Union troops through the South, **General William Tecumseh Sherman** won the battle of **Kennesaw Mountain** in Georgia, and, after the retreating Confederates had torched the city, captured Atlanta in September 1864. He then marched his 100,000 troops 60 miles through the heart of the South, burning and plundering Georgia as he went. His **scorched-earth** policy, which targeted civilians, was aimed at inflicting such misery as would compel the South to surrender. He took Savannah, Georgia, in December of 1864 and Columbia, South Carolina, in February of 1865, as Grant was approaching victory in Virginia.

FORMER SLAVES' CONTRIBUTIONS

President Lincoln eventually credited the 180,000 freed slaves (**freedmen**) who made their way north and fought (in segregated units) in the Union army or worked in supporting jobs with turning the tide of the war, which was partly won on sheer manpower.

The South Surrenders and Lincoln is Assassinated

Jefferson Davis still clung to the dream of Southern independence, but Lincoln would not consider anything but the South's unconditional surrender and restoration of the Union. Surrounded by General Grant's forces and knowing that the end was inevitable, General Lee officially surrendered on the steps of the **Appomattox Court House** on **April 9, 1865.** Five days later, on **April 14, 1865**, as President Lincoln watched a play in **Ford's Theatre** in Washington, D.C., he was assassinated by Southern sympathizer **John Wilkes Booth**. With Lincoln assassinated, Vice President **Andrew Johnson** assumed the presidency in 1865.

The Abolition of Slavery

The Confiscation Acts, passed in the first years of the war, allowed Union troops to seize enemy property (and slaves were still defined as property) that could be used in an act of war. The second of these acts freed slaves in any territory currently in rebellion against the Union. **The Emancipation Proclamation,** issued January 1, 1863, followed the preliminary proclamation of the same name that was issued right after the battle of Antietam. Though it only applied to slaves living in Confederate states, leaving slavery legal in the border states, and did have its critics, the proclamation bolstered the morale of Union troops. **The Thirteenth Amendment** to the Constitution, which granted freedom to slaves in the border states, abolished slavery in the United States. Though Lincoln had worked tirelessly to secure its passage, he did not live to see it ratified in 1865. With the stroke of a pen, the country gained 4 million new citizens.

Other Consequences of the War

Both sides of the reunited nation had lost about 5 percent of the population to injury and death. Women had become heads of households, had taken on jobs in the fields and the factories, and had worked as nurses in battle and as volunteers in veterans' hospitals. Rather than emphasizing states' rights, the new government stressed the preservation of the Union and the supremacy of the federal government. The west had benefited from wartime acts that stimulated settlement at the frontier: the **Homestead Act of 1862** had granted 160 acres to any family that agreed to farm them for at least five years, the **Morrill Land Grant Act of 1862** had given states federal lands to be used for colleges that would educate people about agriculture and the technical trades, and the **Pacific Railway Acts of 1862 and 1864** approved the building of a transcontinental railroad running all the way from the Atlantic Ocean to the Pacific.

THINGS TO REMEMBER

TERMS

House of Representatives	loose constructionist	specie	49ers
Senate	elastic clause	emancipation	Republican Party
Electoral College	compact theory	corrupt bargain	border ruffians
Federalists	midnight judges	pet bank	Constitutional Union Party
Anti-Federalists	writ of mandamus	spoils system	
Bank of the United States	judicial review	kitchen cabinet	Confederate States of America
Democratic-Republicans	impeachment	suffrage	
Barbary Pirates	partisan	Perfectionism	Copperheads
central government	secession	cult of domesticity	freedmen
separation of powers	American System	antebellum	greenbacks
factions	overspeculation	mandate	ironclads
mobocracy	nativists	popular sovereignty	scorched-earth tactics
funding at par	constituents	apologists	writ of habeas corpus
strict constructionist	inflation	Free-Soil Party	agrarian

PEOPLE

John Adams	John Quincy Adams	Joseph Smith	Mormon Church
Thomas Jefferson	Eli Whitney	Brigham Young	transcendentalists
James Madison	Anti-Masons	Ralph Waldo Emerson	Shakers
Lewis and Clark	National Republicans	Henry David Thoreau	Oneida Commune
John Marshall	Whigs	Nathaniel Hawthorne	Knickerbockers
Tecumseh and the Prophet	Robert Hayne	William Lloyd Garrison	Sam Houston
Andrew Jackson	Charles G. Finney	American Temperance Society	James K. Polk
Essex Junto	Dorothea Dix		Harriet Beecher Stowe
American Party	Horace Mann	American Antislavery Society	George Fitzburgh
Know-Nothing Party	Harriet Tubman		John Brown
James Monroe	Sojourner Truth	Liberty Party	Robert E. Lee
John C. Calhoun	Fredrick Douglass	Foreign Antislavery Society	Ulysses S. Grant
Daniel Webster	Sarah and Angelina Grimke	Church of Jesus Christ of Latter-Day Saints	Abraham Lincoln
Henry Clay			John Wilkes Booth

EVENTS

Farewell Address	Tripolitan Wars	The Panic of 1819	New York Draft Riots
Whiskey Rebellion	Napoleonic War	Panic of 1837	Bull Run
XYZ Affair	Battle of Tippecanoe	Southern Carolina Exposition	Second Battle of Bull Run
Convention of 1800	Battle of New Orleans		Antietam
French Revolution	Hartford Convention	Trail of Tears	Gettysburg
Burr Conspiracy	Era of Good Feeling	Nat Turner's Rebellion	

THINGS TO REMEMBER

PLACES

Erie Canal	Seneca Falls	Bleeding Kansas	Appomattox Court House
Underground Railroad	Oregon Trail	Harper's Ferry	

DOCUMENTS

Virginia Plan	Judiciary Act of 1801	Adams-Onis Treaty	Treaty of Guadalupe
New Jersey Plan	Twelfth Amendment	Monroe Doctrine	Hidalgo
Great Compromise	Berlin Decree	*Gibbons v. Ogden*	Webster-Ashburton Treaty
Three-Fifths Compromise	Orders in Council	Specie Circular	Gadsden Purchase
Northwest Ordinance	Milan Decree	Tariff of 1828	Fugitive Slave Law
Bill of Rights	Embargo Act	Tariff of 1832	Compromise of 1850
The Federalist Papers	Non-Intercourse Act	Force Bill	Kansas-Nebraska Act
Judiciary Act of 1789	of 1809	Indian Removal Act	Lecompton Constitution
Report on Public Credit	Macon's Bill Number 2	*Cherokee Nation v. Georgia*	*Dred Scott v. Sanford*
Report on Manufactures	"The Star-Spangled	*Worcester v. Georgia*	Freeport Doctrine
Revenue Act of 1789	Banner"	Maine Law	Anaconda Plan
Neutrality Proclamation	Treaty of Ghent	The North Star	Emancipation Proclamation
of 1793	Tariff of 1816	Declaration of Sentiments	Thirteenth Amendment
Jay's Treaty	Tallmadge Amendment	Walden	Homestead Act of 1862
Alien and Sedition Acts	Missouri Compromise	"On Civil Disobedience"	Morrill Land Grant of 1862
Pinckney Treaty	Rush-Bagot Treaty	Wilmot Proviso	Pacific Railway Act of 1862

Practice Section

1. During the deliberations over ratification, Anti-Federalists claimed that the Constitution

    (A) did not guard individuals and states' civil liberties from the national government.

    (B) should put an end to slavery.

    (C) needed to ensure proportional representation in the legislative branch.

    (D) required the resources for the coinage of money.

    (E) should specify a dominant executive branch.

2. The Kentucky and Virginia Resolutions held that

    (A) the Constitution provided for the organization of a federal bank.

    (B) states were reasonable in declaring federal laws null and void.

    (C) states should be consulted before neutrality was declared.

    (D) the House could settle tied votes in presidential elections.

    (E) the federal government had the right to keep enemies as prisoners during war.

3. The War of 1812 resulted in all of the following EXCEPT

    (A) the elimination of Native American attacks in the Ohio Valley.

    (B) a growing sense of patriotism.

    (C) the development of American commerce and engineering.

    (D) newfound admiration for the United States overseas.

    (E) increasing respect for the Federalist party.

4. The expansion of the American Party in 1849 indicated that

    (A) many Americans were ready to permit the national government to start spending on public works ventures.

    (B) leaders were dissatisfied with the financial choices of Democrats.

    (C) some Americans were apprehensive about the climb in immigration.

    (D) Congress was moving toward abolishing slavery.

    (E) Democrats and Whigs were ready to collaborate to mend the economic structure.

5. The United States in 1850

    (A) included a free black population that resided mainly in the North.

    (B) had very few Americans still making a living through agriculture.

    (C) had a frontier that started west of the Mississippi River.

    (D) had few Native American tribes still in existence.

    (E) included a large working class that was defended by a central government.

6. Andrew Jackson's plan for prolonged democracy is best demonstrated by

    (A) the Force Bill.

    (B) the BUS veto.

    (C) the Indian Removal Act.

    (D) the Specie Circular.

    (E) the South Carolina Exposition.

7. Antebellum reform movements sought to

(A) treat society's evils for the betterment of humanity.

(B) supply individual aid to those who needed it.

(C) develop a democracy that included the underprivileged.

(D) construct a "perfect" American society.

(E) restrict the religious freedom of fragmented spiritual sects.

8. The Mexican War resulted in

(A) closer diplomatic associations between the United States and Mexico.

(B) a decline in arguments over the expansion of slavery.

(C) the annexation of Texas.

(D) the U.S. acquisition of California and territories in the southwest.

(E) an increased sense of isolationism among most U.S. citizens.

9. In spite of being formed by members from various other parties, the Republicans held strong in their conviction that

(A) slavery was ethically immoral.

(B) popular sovereignty was the necessary course of action.

(C) the South had the right to secede from the Union.

(D) slavery should not be legally extended into the territories.

(E) the *Dred Scott* decision was upheld by the Constitution.

10. The Battle of Gettysburg was significant in that

(A) General Lee was conquered.

(B) the Confederates would never have another triumph.

(C) Ulysses S. Grant was able to capture the Mississippi River.

(D) the Confederates successfully crossed the Potomac River.

(E) the port of New Orleans was closed to trade.

Answers and Explanations

1. A

Anti-Federalists were very upset over potential abuses by the federal government and feared that the Constitution did not protect individual and states' rights. They would not ratify the Constitution without the addition of provisions to offer that defense. The addition of the Bill of Rights provided the protections necessary to secure ratification and satisfy the Anti-Federalists.

2. B

To fight the Alien and Sedition Acts, Thomas Jefferson and James Madison each wrote laws in Kentucky and Virginia, respectively, to nullify them. They argued that the federal government had broken its "compact" with the states by failing to protect free speech and they were therefore justified in proclaiming the acts null and void. However, the Alien and Sedition Acts were not officially nullified by any state, although the idea of nullification re-emerged in the regional debates that splintered the Republic before the Civil War.

3. E

After avoiding a war with Britain, the Federalists were labeled as unpatriotic after the War of 1812, thus losing support. Americans emerged from the war more nationalistic due to victories such as the Great Lakes naval battle and the Battle of New Orleans. Native Americans were removed as a threat during the Battle of Tippecanoe and Jackson's other war campaigns. The war helped industry grow and created a sense of respect for the United States overseas.

4. C

The American or Know-Nothing Party was created in response to the massive influx of immigrants from Ireland and Germany. The party eventually disbanded in the mid-1850s due to its refusal to take a stand on the topic of slavery and also due to the rise of the Republican Party.

5. C

The American frontier now began west of the Mississippi River. While the number of Americans involved in industry had grown, agriculture was still the main way of earning a living. Native American tribes had diminished and moved west, but many were still in existence. Approximately 250,000 free blacks lived in the North, but approximately the same number chose to live in the South. The working class did not begin to enjoy the protection of the federal government until the turn of the 20th century.

6. B

Jackson saw the Bank of the United States as a threat to the well-being and success of the common man. To expand democracy and end an institution he saw as corrupt, Jackson vowed to kill the BUS before it could be rechartered.

7. D

While on the surface, antebellum reformers looked as though they were simply working to foster a better society, it was a "perfect" society they were after. Middle-class Americans felt their peaceful way of life threatened by the excesses of the wealthy and the desperation of the poor and thus sought ways to insulate themselves from these perceived dangers.

8. D

The Mexican government ceded California and the territory that now makes up the states of Arizona, New Mexico, Utah, and Nevada to the United States under the Treaty of Guadalupe-Hidalgo in 1848. Texas had already been annexed by the United States in 1846. Mexicans held a deep resentment toward Americans for some time after the war. As Americans were emboldened by their victory, they sought other opportunities for expansion, which further fueled the tensions over slavery.

9. D

Part of the broad appeal of the Republican platform was its stance regarding the nonextension of slavery into the territories. Not all Republicans agreed upon the moral nature of slavery or the effectiveness of popular sovereignty.

10. B

Unfortunately for General Lee and his Confederate compatriots, the bloody Battle of Gettysburg signaled the end of their winning streak. Suffering great losses and unable to launch a strong enough flanking maneuver, Lee was forced to retreat to Virginia.

CHAPTER 3

Post–Civil War Reconstruction through World War I: 1877–1919

❯❯ THE TRIALS OF RECONSTRUCTION: 1863–1877

Rebuilding the Nation

TEN PERCENT PLAN

The rebuilding of the nation required federal intervention. The 1863 **Proclamation of Amnesty and Reconstruction,** also known as Lincoln's **10% Plan**, required that at least 10 percent of a state's population swear loyalty to the country and the Constitution before re-establishing that state's government. This plan allowed complete pardons to all former confederates who took the oath of allegiance to eliminate slavery.

> ### ▶ AP EXPERT TIP
>
> Avoid interference from other subjects by making U.S. History the one you study right before you go to sleep.

WADE-DAVIS BILL

This readmission bill required 50 percent of Southern state voters to swear that they had never supported the Confederacy *and* swear loyalty to the United States. Though Congress passed it in 1864, Lincoln pocket-vetoed (procedurally killed) it.

THE FREEDMAN'S BUREAU

Set up by President Lincoln in 1865 to give food, shelter, and medical aid to freed slaves and southern whites and set up schools to educate former slaves across the South, this agency died in 1872 after President Johnson refused to fund it. Johnson also opposed an earlier war initiative of General Sherman to give every freed slave **40 acres and a mule**. Conciliatory towards Southerners, Johnson kept the 10% Plan. In the 1866 congressional election, radicalized Republicans gained a two-thirds majority in both houses. While Congress was not in session, Southern legislatures adopted the **Black Codes,** which prevented African Americans from owning land. Ex-slaves could lease land and borrow supplies from white landowners to become **sharecroppers**. They had to pay so much from their harvests that they were perpetually in debt.

RADICAL REPUBLICANS SET OUT TO PROTECT FREED SLAVES WITH NEW LEGISLATION

The Civil Rights Bill of 1866, which the Republican Congress passed into law over the president's veto, gave blacks full citizenship. The Republicans then wrote and later ratified a new constitutional amendment that would protect the Civil Rights Bill from being undone if the Democrats gained a congressional majority. **The Fourteenth Amendment** protected all U.S. citizens' rights, required all states to adhere to the Constitution's due process and equal protection clauses, barred ex-Confederate officers from state or federal office, and decreased the proportional representation of any state denying suffrage to any able citizen. Congress tightened its power over the South by establishing martial law in former Confederate states through the **Military Reconstruction Act of 1867,** and it required former Confederate states to ratify the Fourteenth Amendment and grant universal male suffrage before rejoining the Union. In 1868, Johnson was impeached by the House of Representatives for dismissing his Secretary of War, Edwin Stanton, in violation of **The Tenure of Office Act** (1867), which Johnson opposed. The conflict had much to do with the simmering hostility of the Radical Republicans toward Johnson, who was acquitted by the Senate by one vote.

THE PRESIDENCY OF ULYSSES S. GRANT, 1869–1877

Aided by the African American vote, General Grant, a war hero and a Republican, won the presidency. Republicans in Congress then set to work to protect the African American vote through another constitutional amendment. Though Grant's administration was plagued by scandals—the most famous were the **Black Friday** scandal, in which James Fisk and Jay Gould used connections to Grant to corner the gold market, and the **Crédit Moblier** scam, where bribes were exchanged for railroad construction contracts—Grant remained popular through his two terms.

THE FIFTEENTH AMENDMENT

This Amendment barred states from denying citizens the right to vote on the basis of race, color, or previous servitude and barred public institutions from denying full and equal use of their premises. Unfortunately, it contained no wording that provided for its enforcement, and after passage it was ignored by most states.

Realities of the Postwar South

All the old era Southerners were Democrats. Southern Republicans (derisively called **scalawags**) composed of freedmen and Northerners who had come to live in the region did gain some strength. The Northerners were called **carpetbaggers,** and were deeply resented. Republican Southern legislatures created state-funded public education and improved or rebuilt roads, rail lines, waterways, hospitals, and prisons, funding them through improved tax codes and collection services.

Southern Democrats created the **Klu Klux Klan** (**KKK**), a secret society aimed at ridding the South of Republicans through terrorist tactics that targeted all of them, black *and* white. Congress tried to abolish the KKK through the **Force Acts of 1870 and 1871,** which authorized the use of federal troops to quell violence and enforce the Fourteenth and Fifteenth Amendments. After this, some Democrats known as **Redeemers** promised voters in the Deep South that they could remove corrupt Republicans and create a revived, industrialized South. By 1870, the Republican Party was dead in the South.

Among the vast church networks that connected black families across the South, it was rumored that the whole state of Kansas had been reserved for black settlers. About 25,000 former slaves known as **Exodusters** began setting out towards Kansas.

The Compromise of 1877

Republican Rutherford B. Hayes gained the presidency in exchange for the end of martial law. To have the presidency, Republicans had to agree to pull federal troops from South Carolina, Florida, and Louisiana, ending martial law in the South and Reconstruction in the United States. The Republican Party, which wanted to protect the rights of freed slaves and dismantle the social structure of the prewar South, became the instrument through which the postwar South was revived.

❯ THE CLOSING OF THE FRONTIER: 1865–1900

Identity and the Frontier

According to **Frederick Jackson Turner's Frontier Thesis** (1893), American character had been shaped by interactions with the frontier. Three new industries (mining, cattle, and farming) beckoned individuals westward. **The Gold Rush** began in 1848, when gold was discovered at **Sutter's Mill** in central California and thousands of adventurous young men (**"49ers"**) rushed to the region to seek their fortunes. As the cities of San Francisco and Sacramento sprang up, a flood of Chinese people left their country to gather wealth in California, but instead of gold to bring home, they found prejudice and poverty. They toiled on the transcontinental railroad, became house servants for the wealthy, or ran laundries for miners' families. When panning for gold was replaced by deep core mining, the environment suffered. In Texas, Kansas, and Nebraska, miles of open grassland became vast cattle ranches when improved rail lines made it practical to transport beef. Ranchers grew rich as hired cowboys and vaqueros moved Texas Longhorn cattle on **"long drives"** from Texas to far away out-of-state junctions. As homesteaders and sheepherders settled down and fenced off the grasslands on which the cattle had grazed, the long drives and their cowboys became the past.

The Plains Tribes Lose Land and Identities

In 1865, 400,000 generally nomadic Native Americans lived freely in the trans-Mississippi west. After the aggressive nonnative Sioux took much of the upper Midwest, the Pawnee asked the federal government to protect them from the Sioux. The government assigned areas to each tribe without understanding the leadership systems or nomadic natures of the tribes, dooming this **reservation** system to failure. At Sand Creek, Colorado, a U.S. militia slaughtered 400 unarmed natives who had been promised protection. Around 1874, **Colonel George Custer** claimed to have found gold within the Sioux reservation in the Black Hills of South Dakota. When a hoard of gold seekers followed, the angry Sioux killed Custer and his men and were hunted down by the white army in return. Helen Jackson's 1881 book, *A Century of Dishonor,* sparked debate about the treatment of Native Americans.

THE DAWES SEVERALTY ACT OF 1887

This federal act stripped tribes of official recognition and legally given land rights and destroyed tribal organization. Native families who "behaved" for 25 years would be given land and citizenship. Reservation land was sold to fund "civilizing" ventures, such as schools that taught Indians to dress and act like whites. In response to forced assimilation, tribes tried to revive their cultures. When the Sioux **Ghost Dance**, created to support this goal, frightened whites, it was outlawed. In 1890, the army tried to stop the Sioux dancing. The **Battle of Wounded Knee**, in which 200 Sioux were slaughtered, was the result.

The Struggles of the New South

Tobacco farming put the South back on its feet, while cheap labor and raw cotton made it a leader in the textile industry. So many farmers decided to grow cotton that they glutted the worldwide market and drove the price to an all-time low in the 1890s. Small farmers could not pay their debts and lost their land. Other tenant farmers were driven off land because the landowner needed to till it. Most farmers, who paid for goods on credit, had to pay back those loans from their next harvest. Poor harvests drove these farmers farther into debt.

PLESSY V FERGUSON AND JIM CROW LAWS

The Supreme Court dismantled Reconstruction protections in 1883, ruling that Congress could not bar private citizens from practicing discrimination. In 1896, in the landmark case *Plessy v Ferguson,* a man who was seven-eighths white refused to give up his "whites-only" seat on a Louisiana railcar and was arrested. He sued, claiming that his civil rights had been violated. When the Supreme Court ruled that because the State of Louisiana had provided a **separate but equal** car for people of color, it thus had not violated the Fourteenth Amendment, the Court made it permissible to discriminate by color in all public places. **Jim Crow Laws,** which segregated public facilities, sprang up across the South. These states also disenfranchised blacks by means of literacy tests, poll taxes, and **grandfather clauses** that only allowed men whose grandfathers had voted before 1865 (before Reconstruction) to vote. Whites were given trial by jury; for blacks, there was **lynching**—unauthorized execution done by a mob.

FARMERS STRUGGLE FOR SURVIVAL

Half a million families were lured to the Great Plains by the **Homestead Act of 1862,** which promised 160 acres of land to those who would first settle and work them for five years. Unfortunately, the drought-ridden terrain forced about two-thirds of the homesteaders out. Those who remained (**sodbusters**) lived a hard life, plagued by drought and insects, in houses built of sod.

FARMING BECOMES BIG BUSINESS

Large-scale **agribusiness** drove family farms out of business. As railroad owners and middlemen made huge profits by eating up the profits of small growers, the **National Grange of Patrons of Husbandry**, a Midwestern farmers' organization, took action. By the mid-1870s, Grangers were organizing farm cooperatives that cut out middlemen by selling farm products directly to buyers. They monitored the railroads and silo owners who charged outrageous prices to ship and store grain. In the *Munn v. Illinois* case of 1877, the Supreme Court ruled that states could regulate the practices of businesses serving the public interest—which certainly applied to railroad rates. However, because federal laws protected interstate commerce, many farmer-friendly laws were overturned. Congress pitched in with the **Interstate Commerce Act of 1887.** This created the **Interstate Commerce Commission (ICC)** to regulate railroad companies' business.

❯❯ THE RISE OF INDUSTRY: 1865–1900

Industrialism and Capitalism

THE GROWTH OF RAILROADS AND THE RISE OF THE RAILROAD BARONS

The U.S. government subsidized the building of the **transcontinental railroad** and gave huge land grants to participating rail companies. **Cornelius Vanderbilt** consolidated and connected a number of isolated eastern rail lines, using uniformly sized gauge steel rails, to create the **New York Central Railroad**. Congress appointed the Union Pacific and Central Pacific Railroad companies to build the western half of the transcontinental railroad. **Leland Stanford** led the **Central Pacific Railroad**. Its Chinese laborers (**Coolies**) completed the treacherous line from Sacramento, California, through the Sierra Nevada Mountains. The **Union Pacific** began its portion of the railroad at Council Bluffs, Iowa, and built on westward with the help of Irish workers (**Paddies**). The Pacific rail lines finally merged at **Promontory Point**, Utah, in May of 1869. The transcontinental railroad was the greatest American technological achievement of its century.

ROBBER BARONS

Capitalists such as Jay Gould inflated their companies' stock values before selling the stock to the public, pocketed the profits, and then let the companies go bankrupt. Dishonest practices such as **pools** (secret arrangements between competing rail companies, which divided up business territories, artificially fixed shipping rates, and split the profits among themselves) flourished among railroad companies. The earlier Supreme Court decision in *Munn v. Illinois* was overturned by the Court with its *Wabash v Illinois* decision in 1886, in which the Court deemed corporations to be "citizens" under the Constitution, thus protecting them (under the Fourteenth Amendment's equal protection clause) from federal regulation.

THE BIRTH OF THE STEEL AND OIL INDUSTRIES

The United States shifted from light manufacturing to heavy industry and experienced a **second Industrial Revolution**, with the steel, oil, and heavy machinery industries in the lead. Steel was central in railroad construction and could be efficiently produced via the **Bessemer process**. By the 1880s, Andrew Carnegie's **Carnegie Steel Company** was producing half of the world's steel. His success was also due to a business tactic he called **vertical integration**, which involved single-handedly controlling every aspect of the steel production process, from mining the ore to distributing final products to customers. He later sold his company to **J. P. Morgan**, who created **U.S. Steel** and made it a billion-dollar corporation. Carnegie went on as a philanthropist, using his immense fortune to establish universities, endow libraries, and promote cultural events.

In 1859, oil had been discovered in the Pennsylvania hills. **John D. Rockefeller** saw potential in **"black gold"** and turned a small petroleum company into a massive monopoly through his business strategy of **horizontal integration**. More damaging to competition than vertical integration, it concentrated on controlling one aspect of the production process, the refining stage. Through consolidation, his **Standard Oil Company** eventually controlled 95 percent of U.S. refineries. He offered stockholders of competing oil companies the opportunity to sell him their shares of stock and control in exchange for **trust** certificates. The board of trustees would then control the companies whose stock they had purchased, and they drove other competitors out of business by cornering the market and pushing prices dramatically downward. Smaller companies were either aggressively acquired or driven out of business. After the **Panic of 1893** threw several railroads into financial ruin, J. P. Morgan and several other Wall Street financiers took over those rail lines and merged them into single companies. However, Morgan dominated the governing boards of these companies. He created **"interlocking directorates,"** regional monopolies that controlled almost two-thirds of the rail traffic in the United States.

LAISSEZ-FAIRE CAPITALISM

Standing by the doctrine of **laissez-faire** articulated by economist **Adam Smith** in his treatise *The Wealth of Nations,* American lawmakers believed that natural market forces, not governments, should regulate the marketplace. However, Congress eventually enacted the **Sherman Antitrust Act** in 1890 to break up the massive monopolies that ruled the economy. In 1895, the Supreme Court, in *United States v. E. C. Knight* ruled that the Constitution's commerce clause did not apply to manufacturing (cutting Congress' power to regulate it) and drastically weakened the Sherman Act.

The Economic/Social Divide Widens

Ninety percent of America's wealth was controlled by 10 percent of the population. The newly wealthy were scornfully called **"nouveau riche"** by the old upper classes. Americans applied **Charles Darwin's** notion of "**survival of the fittest**" to economic matters, and **social Darwinism** was born. Many lower-class Americans also subscribed to the **"rags-to-riches"** myth, as popularized in **Horatio Alger's** novels.

THE TRICKLE-DOWN THEORY

This theory of economics proposed that great wealth in the hands of a few was of great benefit to all of society, since it would **trickle down** to the rest of society as the rich spent it. Andrew Carnegie, a proponent of the trickle-down theory, wrote *The Gospel of Wealth*, claiming that since wealth was God's will, the wealthy had an obligation to give money away to better society.

Labor Organizes

The increased demand for cheap manufactured goods was hard on American factory workers, who often moved from day to night shifts, working 24 hours straight. When American laborers organized for better wages and safer working conditions, they met with resistance. If they went on strike, cheap replacement laborers (**scabs**) were hired, and private police forces dealt violently with the strikers. Strikes were also prevented through **lockouts**. New hires were required to sign **yellow-dog contracts** or "**ironclad oaths**" that they would not join unions. One of the earliest and most violently resisted protests, the **Great Railroad Strike of 1877**, occurred after rail companies cut wages by 10 percent. Over 100 men died after President Hayes called in troops to break the strike.

UNIONS ATTEMPT TO PROTECT RIGHTS

The first union, the **National Labor Union**, was founded in 1866 to promote better working conditions, higher wages, shorter hours, and the inclusion of women and African Americans in the workforce, but it died after the 1877 Railroad Strike. The secretly formed **Knights of Labor**, another inclusive union, emerged in the early 1880s: it included Granger-style labor cooperatives, an eight-hour workday, government regulation of business, and arbitration as a means of settling disputes between labor and management. Unfortunately, after someone in the crowd threw a bomb that killed eight policemen during an 1886 Knights of Labor protest in Chicago's **Haymarket Square**, it was alleged that the Knights were part of an anarchist movement. Many former Knights joined **Samuel Gompers** and his **American Federation of Labor (AFL)**, which became the country's largest union. The AFL was a practical union of over a million members. Using collective bargaining, it obtained modest gains for workers by founding **closed shops** (businesses in which all employees had to belong to the union).

A STRIKEBREAKING GOVERNMENT

One facet of the government's support of big business was the practice of strikebreaking. In 1892, Henry Frick, the manager of Andrew Carnegie's Homestead Steel mill, cut worker wages by 20 percent and locked out union members to prevent a strike. Sixteen people died and over 150 were wounded in the melee that followed. When the **Pullman Palace Car Company**, which manufactured railroad sleeping cars, cut wages and fired the employee union leader, Pullman workers stopped working and sought the help of the American Railway Union under the leadership of **Eugene V. Debs**. Rail workers across the nation refused to load, link, or carry any train that had a Pullman car attached. In response, the rail owners hitched U.S. mail cars to Pullman cars so that they could claim that the strikers were impeding the flow of mail, thus violating the laws protecting interstate commerce. President Cleveland backed an antistrike injunction filed to restore the flow of mail. After Debs and his union refused to abide by the court's ruling, they were arrested and jailed. With the subsequent Supreme Court ruling in *In re Debs* (1895) that court injunctions breaking strikes were justified in support of interstate commerce, the federal government gave employers permission to destroy labor unions.

❯ FROM A RURAL TO AN URBAN AMERICA: 1865–1900

More Immigrants Arrive

Immigrants flocked to cities to find cheap housing and abundant factory jobs. Ethnic ghettos popped up in New York, Chicago, and Philadelphia. Airshafts intended to distribute fresh air through the apartments of "**dumbbell tenements**" actually spread infectious diseases through the overcrowded buildings. As the inner cities changed and expanded, trolley and subway services made commuting possible and middle-class white Americans moved to burgeoning suburbia.

The Rise of Urban Political Machines

Large, consolidated political groups called "**machines**" controlled party politics in such cities as New York, Chicago, and Baltimore. They traded coveted city jobs for votes, found housing for newly arrived immigrants, and doled out various forms of support to needy families. New York City's famous **Tammany Hall** machine was led by Irish American "**Boss" Tweed**. Practicing what they called "**honest graft**," Tammany Hall bosses would learn of proposed city projects from insiders on the planning board, buy the land intended for the site, then sell it to the city at two or three times the original price. By 1870, the Tweed ring had bilked New York City taxpayers of over $200 million. Though city dwellers who were cared for and protected by the machines did not complain, Tweed fell from power after Tammany Hall's corruption and greed was exposed by the press. He died in jail in 1878.

New Waves of Social Reform and Cultural Awakenings

SOCIAL REFORM MOVEMENTS

Walter Rauschenbusch, who believed that Christians had an obligation to further social improvement, led the influential **Social Gospel Movement** from the rough Hell's Kitchen area of New York City. Without a voice in the political process, a number of young, college-educated, middle-class female activists founded the **Settlement House Movement** to better society through volunteerism. Chicago's famous **Hull House,** which brought immigrants and the poor in to live with college-educated people and gain skill in English, hygiene, and childcare, became the model for other institutions.

THE CHANGING ROLES OF WOMEN

Francis Willard and the **Woman's Christian Temperance Union (WCTU)** believed that prohibition would cure society of such ills as poverty. **The Anti-Saloon League** followed in 1893. During Reconstruction, the issue of African American suffrage had taken precedence over women's suffrage. The cause was revived as women's suffrage groups were formed from the 1870s to the 1890s. Activists **Elizabeth Cady Stanton** and **Susan B. Anthony** formed the **National American Woman Suffrage Association** in 1890 by getting the National Woman Suffrage Association and the American Woman Suffrage Association to merge and fight for a woman's right to vote. Gains came slowly, but they did come. By 1900, a number of western states had provisions for women to vote.

CHANGES IN EDUCATION

Publicly funded high schools and compulsory elementary attendance laws brought America's literacy rate close to 90 percent. Already supplemented by the **Hatch Act of 1887**, higher education received new funds from men such as Carnegie, Rockefeller, Stanford, and Vanderbilt. American universities created "social science" by applying the scientific method to social disciplines, and they professionalized medicine, law, and sociology with strengthened degree requirements. "Normal" schools (teachers' colleges) were established across the country.

ACHIEVEMENTS IN THE ARTS

Leaving romanticism behind, **realist writers and artists** sought to portray America as it was. **Mark Twain** named the era "**the Gilded Age**" and wrote of the frontier and the South with humor and satire. **Bret Harte** wrote of the gold rush and Wild West.

Painters such as **Winslow Homer** followed the Hudson River School's romantic spirit through lush American land- and seascapes, while others such as **James Whistler** and **Mary Cassatt** broke from tradition and changed America's perception of color and composition through their works.

Frederick Law Olmsted brought nature to the city by designing vast parks that were densely planted and meticulously planned. His **Central Park** in New York City set the standard.

African American music moved to Northern cities from the Deep South. In the 1890s early **jazz**, known as **ragtime**, became the rage and took on local peculiarities as it moved from city to city. The nation danced to **Scott Joplin**'s "Maple Leaf Rag." **Booker T. Washington**, a former slave, founded the Tuskegee Institute to teach African Americans the industrial arts.

Informing and entertaining the masses was now big business in cities such as New York and Chicago. Daily newspapers like **Joseph Pulitzer's** *The New York World* and **William Randolph Hearst's** *New York Journal* fought for circulation with sensationalized stories. Magazines such as *Ladies' Home Journal, McCall's,* and *Vogue* attracted women readers with glittery advertisements and fashion tips. In the South, **minstrel shows**, where white actors in blackface mimicked African Americans, were popular among both whites and blacks.

❯❯ POPULISTS AND PROGRESSIVES: 1890–1919

"Forgettable Administrations": The Rutherford B. Hayes, James Garfield, and Chester A. Arthur Years, 1877–1885

Post-Reconstruction politics were marked by three lackluster presidents who served one term apiece. Republicans were split into three factions. Republican **Stalwarts** opposed their **Halfbreed** colleagues, while the **Mugwumps** (Republicans who supported Democrats) took the middle ground on issues. The patronage system tainted Rutherford B. Hayes's unremarkable presidency from 1877–1881. As Halfbreed President James Garfield appointed party loyalists to coveted civil service positions, he ignored the strong Stalwart contingency, one of whom shot him in the back in 1881. Garfield died from the wound three months later, and his Stalwart vice president assumed office. Once he became president in 1881, Chester A. Arthur began to separate himself from his Stalwart pals.

The Pendleton Civil Service Act of 1881 reformed the corrupt patronage system by requiring all potential civil service employees to take an exam to prove their worth. Issues regarding currency and the high protective tariff provoked disputes that would carry over to the 1888 election. The Greenback Party thought that paper money not backed by hard specie (coins) would solve the economic woes.

Grover Cleveland's First Term (Democrat), 1885–1889

Cleveland became the first Democrat to win the executive office since pre–Civil War days. As agrarian discontent grew, he supported lowering the tariff to benefit southern and western farmers. Displeasing northern business owners, this stance cost him the next term.

The Benjamin Harrison Administration (Republican), 1889–1893

Drawing on the earlier Grange movement, farmers in several states joined forces to form the **Farmers' Alliance**, which gained enough support to produce senators and governors in several Midwestern states before becoming the **Populist (People's) Party**. In 1892 in Omaha, Nebraska, the Populists drafted a political platform which called for the unlimited coinage of silver; a graduated income tax; public ownership of the railroads, telegraph, and telephone companies; government subsidies to stabilize agricultural prices; and an eight-hour workday. They supported the direct election of U.S. senators and increased voter power through the use of initiatives, referendums, and recalls. Though the Populists made an impressive showing against the other presidential candidates (President Harrison and former President Cleveland) and garnered 1 million popular (and 22 electoral) votes, they failed to win the election.

Cleveland's Second Term (Democrat), 1893–1897

Though Grover Cleveland became the only president to win a second term after having left office, his victory celebration would be short. **The Panic of 1893** gave way to depression after stock prices, inflated by overspeculation, plunged downward. The market did not recover for almost four years. To mitigate the crisis, President Cleveland brokered a $65 million loan from wealthy investment banker J. P. Morgan and repealed the Sherman Silver Purchase Act (1890), which increased the amount of silver the government was required to buy. Protesters marched on the Capitol, where Populist **Jacob Coxey**'s **"army"** of the jobless and the homeless asked the government to fund public works projects, which could then employ those who needed work.

GOLD VERSUS SILVER IN THE 1896 ELECTION

The Democrats were split on the gold and silver controversy, with **"Gold Bugs"** such as Cleveland on one side and leaderless pro-silver advocates on the other. After **William Jennings Bryan** of Nebraska spoke up for the pro-silver advocates in his famous **"Cross of Gold"** speech at the Democratic National Convention, the Democrats made him their candidate and essentially adopted the old Populist platform as their own. Cleveland and his "Gold Bugs" were disgusted with the new party's direction and left to form their own splinter group. The Republicans nominated gold standard proponent **William McKinley**.

William McKinley (Republican), 1897–1901

As the economy took an upturn, world events began drawing American's attention away from domestic issues. McKinley was assassinated in his second term. The killer, Leon Czolgosz, had been influenced by anarchist rhetoric.

Theodore Roosevelt Presidency (Republican), 1901–1909

McKinley's spirited, progressive vice president, Theodore Roosevelt, became the nation's leader. The first **"modern president"** who actively set an agenda for Congress and expected it to listen to his suggestions, he was also known as a **Progressive president**.

Reform movements had already set firm roots in local and state politics (in 1888, Massachusetts' voters had begun to vote by **secret ballots**), but when young Teddy Roosevelt became president, the spirit of change gained a national audience. Initiated in 1901, the Progressive Era continued through 1917. Most progressives were white, middle-class Protestants who wanted reform to better society.

MUCKRAKING JOURNALISTS AND AUTHORS STIR CONTROVERSY

As newspaper giants **Pulitzer** and **Hearst** drew in readers with sensational stories, **"muckraker"** authors and journalists wrote articles, essays, and books that exposed scandal, corruption, and injustice. The muckrakers gained large audiences and stirred up concerns among readers through such magazines as *McClure's* and *Collier's*. *The History of the Standard Oil Company*, a 1902 series by **Ida Tarbell**, brought John D. Rockefeller's ruthless business tactics to light and caused quite a stir. Danish photojournalist **Jacob Riis**'s 1890 volume *How the Other Half Lives* presented photographs of life in the tenements of New York City's **Lower East Side** neighborhood.

STATE AND LOCAL PROGRESSIVISM

Wisconsin became the first state in the Union to institute direct primaries. The state's voters could nominate their own slate of candidates. This **Wisconsin Experiment** also set the tone for other states, which reformed laws related to taxation, representation, and regulation of commerce. State and local voters could also propose a law directly (without the legislature) by means of an *initiative*, put a proposed law on the ballot as a *referendum*, or try to remove an elected official from office by initiating a *recall*. Citizens' voices were heard and their wishes made law as the part of **the Seventeenth Amendment to the Constitution,** which enabled voters to elect their U.S. senators directly.

City governments also privatized public entities, such as departments of water, power, and transportation, to get them out of the grip of corrupt political machines. As the nation's first municipality to appoint a city planning commission, Galveston, Texas, became a model of reform.

PRESIDENTIAL PROGRESSIVISM: ROOSEVELT'S SQUARE DEAL

The **Square Deal** aimed to bust harmful trusts, increase government regulation of big business, and promote conservation of the natural environment. When Roosevelt threatened to take over the mines during the 1902 anthracite coal strike in Pennsylvania and run them with federal troops, the mine owners agreed to lift their lockout, offer workers a 10 percent pay raise, and give in to a nine-hour workday.

Averting a national calamity helped Roosevelt get re-elected in his own right in 1904. He fought the **Northern Securities Company** railroad trust all the way to the Supreme Court, which ruled on his side. He gained further railroad industry regulation through 1903's **Elkins Act**, which gave the **Interstate Commerce Commission** more power to prohibit rail companies from giving rebates and kickbacks to favored customers, and 1906's **Hepburn Act**, which let the ICC regulate railroad shipping rates. Roosevelt also sought to wipe out "harmful" trusts, such as Standard Oil. Roosevelt pushed to get the **Pure Food and Drug Act** and the **Meat Inspection Act** passed in 1906. **Conservation of the environment** was another piece of Roosevelt's "Square Deal." An ardent outdoorsman, Roosevelt preserved millions of acres of land through the creation of the **National Conservation Commission** and the **Antiquities Act** (1906), which allowed the government to protect historic landmarks such as Devils Tower in Wyoming.

William Taft Presidency (Republican), 1909–1913

Taft, who had been Roosevelt's secretary of war, continued dismantling trusts and protecting natural resources. **The Mann-Elkins Act** of 1910 authorized the Interstate Commerce Commission (ICC) to regulate communication. **The Sixteenth Amendment to the Constitution,** ratified during his presidency, allowed the federal government to collect income tax. However, Taft's party was split, with liberal progressives on one side and conservative "Old Guard" Republicans on the other. When Taft further angered Teddy Roosevelt by prosecuting U.S. Steel for carrying out a merger that Roosevelt himself had approved, the former president responded by running for president again in the 1912 election.

The Woodrow Wilson Presidency (Democrat), 1913–1921

Taft was the Republican candidate, Theodore Roosevelt ran as a **Progressive Republican** (or "**Bull Moose**"), and political newcomer **Woodrow Wilson** became the Democratic contender. The Socialists ran **Eugene V. Debs**. Roosevelt introduced his "**New Nationalism**," under which government would regulate business, women would vote, and federal welfare programs would be offered to the poorest Americans. Wilson countered with his "**New Freedom**," which promised a smaller, reformed government less influenced by big business and more supportive of small businesses. With the Republican Party split, Wilson won without being able to claim a mandate.

A Progressive Democrat, Wilson sought to break what he saw as the "**triple wall of privilege**": high tariffs, unfair banking practices, and monopolies by trusts. He persuaded Congress to pass the **Underwood Tariff Bill** in 1913. This lowered the price people had to pay for manufactured goods while offsetting the loss of tariff revenues with a permanent federal income tax on wealthier citizens. From then on, the government's tax revenues would exceed its revenues from tariffs.

Still concerned about the financial health of the nation, Wilson asked Congress to address the problem of the money supply. Congress responded with the monumental **Federal Reserve Act**, which created the **Federal Reserve System** in 1913. This new banking system consisted of 12 regional banks that were publicly *controlled* by the new **Federal Reserve Board** but privately *owned* by member banks. The system would serve as the "**lender of last resort**" for all private banks, hold or sell the nation's bonds, and issue **Federal Reserve Notes** (dollar bills). For first time since Andrew Jackson killed the Second Bank of the United States, the country would have a national bank. Passed in 1913, the **Clayton Antitrust Act** (hailed as the "**Magna Carta of Labor**") strengthened the Sherman Antitrust Act with provisions for breaking up trusts and protecting labor unions from prosecution. In 1914, Wilson created the **Federal Trade Commission,** a regulatory agency that monitors business activities and forces lawbreaking companies to comply with "cease and desist" orders.

Women's Suffrage

Many women entered the factories as textile workers in spinning mills or large garment factories. Others became telephone or telegraph operators, secretaries, or typists. As the "lesser sex" took on these jobs, the pay was decreased. Some women entered the world of academia when women's colleges such as Mount Holyoke, Wellesley, and Barnard offered them liberal arts educations. The **International Ladies' Garment Workers Union (ILGWU)** organized female sweatshop workers. After the **Triangle Shirtwaist Factory** fire of 1911 claimed 146 employees' lives, the ILGWU spread word of the tragedy. Emboldened by the success of male Progressives, college-educated women looked to improve their standing as well. **Carrie Chapman Catt**, president of the **National American Woman Suffrage Association (NAWSA)**, was an outspoken advocate of women's suffrage. In 1913, **Alice Paul** formed the **National Woman's Party**, which picketed the White House and the Capitol demanding the vote. President Wilson publicly supported the **Nineteenth Amendment,** which granted women the right to vote, and it was signed into law in 1920. Catt formed the **League of Women Voters**, while Paul continued with the National Woman's Party.

African Americans at the Turn of the Century

Progressives were interested in preserving *their* way of life from the wickedness of poverty, drunkenness, and corruption, not in helping blacks. Progressive President Wilson even segregated federal buildings. When Reconstruction ended, black civil rights ended with it. **Booker T. Washington** argued that blacks needed to work within the white world and had to succeed economically to become equal to whites, a view that came to be known as "**accommodation,**" while Harvard-educated **W. E. B. DuBois** wanted African Americans to demand social and political equality first. DuBois's **Niagara Movement** joined other African Americans and concerned whites to form the **National Association for the Advancement of Colored People (NAACP)** on February 12, 1908. As the NAACP developed into one of the largest and most active civil rights groups in the country, it became influential enough to push President Wilson to condemn lynching publicly in 1918. Between 1910 and 1930, a "**Great Migration**" of millions of African Americans left the South for northern cities. Lured to the cities by promises of factory work and less discrimination, blacks wound up living in ghettos, working at low-paying jobs, and experiencing racial conflict.

❯ FOREIGN POLICY: 1865–1919

A New Imperialism

With the closing of the western frontier, many Americans felt that Manifest Destiny had still not been fulfilled. Many wanted to expand beyond the contiguous United States. After Secretary of State William H. Seward brokered the **Alaska Purchase** and the United States paid Russia $7.2 million for the land in 1867, Alaska was called "**Seward's**

Folly" or "**Seward's Icebox**." Not until the 20th century would Americans realize the sweet deal they had received when oil drillers found that Alaska was rich with fossil fuel.

In the name of social Darwinism, Imperialists justified expansionism in the late 19th and early 20th centuries. Americans had removed the Native Americans from the west so easily that it seemed natural to remove native populations overseas in the name of "progress." Armed with the concept of **jingoism** (extreme nationalism that encourages a very aggressive foreign policy stance), U.S. Naval Captain Alfred Thayer Mahan's influential book *The Influence of Sea Power upon History* (1890) proposed that the United States build a world-class navy in order to become a major world power broker, occupy sites (such as Hawaii and Cuba) around the world to use as refueling stations and naval bases, and create a shortcut from the Pacific to the Atlantic by building a canal across the Isthmus of Panama. Early expansionists had focused on Pacific islands and Central America.

As unauthorized U.S. troops landed on the **Hawaiian Islands** to assist pineapple exporter Sanford B. Dole fight queen Liliuokalani in 1893, the U.S. Minister to Hawaii said, "The Hawaiian pear is now fully ripe, and this is the golden hour for the United States to pluck it." By the time President Cleveland learned of the incursion, a treaty to authorize the annexation of the islands had already reached Congress. Cleveland refused to sign it. In 1894, Dole and his followers declared Hawaii an independent republic. Hopes of annexation faded until 1898, when Dole was appointed to serve as territorial governor of the islands.

The Spanish American War, April–August, 1898

The debate regarding overseas expansionism turned to the Spanish-held island of Cuba. After the Civil War, Americans had established large sugar plantations on the island. When Cubans grew increasingly irritated by the American and Spanish foreigners who amassed huge fortunes while they toiled to subsist on the plantations, the Spanish decided to nip a revolution in the bud. Cubans died as the Spaniards "re-concentrated" them into central locations under direct Spanish control.

As word of this got to Americans via the sensationalist "yellow journalism" press, Americans and Cuban immigrants in the United States grew concerned, as did American jingoists. In 1898, in a letter leaked to Hearst's *Journal*, the Spanish minister to the United States insinuated that President McKinley was corrupt. The **USS** *Maine*, which had arrived in Havana Harbor to provide protection and act as an escape vessel for the Americans living on the island, exploded under mysterious circumstances while at anchor, killing 260 sailors and injuring many more. Though the Spanish denied any role in the event, Americans found evidence that a submarine mine had sunk the ship. Hearst and Pulitzer published the allegations in the United States. Americans now cried, "Remember the Maine!" as they pushed for war with Spain. Not a jingoist, President McKinley added the **Teller Amendment,** which stated that the United States intended to grant Cuba independence after the war ended, to the declaration of war.

The Spanish-American War began in 1898 and took place in the Spanish colony of the Philippines. The U.S. Navy opened fire on Manila Bay on May 1 and routed the Spanish fleet in a matter of days. But the battle on land was not as easy. Many Filipinos fought against the Spanish *and* the American forces. Only after Filipino revolutionary Emilio Aguinaldo was persuaded to assist in the fight against the Spanish in exchange for independence after the war's end were the Americans, working with Filipino fighters, able to take Manila in August.

Tropical diseases and American inexperience made the fight in Cuba much more difficult. Of 5,000 American deaths, only 10 percent were from combat injuries; most resulted from diseases and food poisoning. In the celebrated American battle for the high ground of San Juan Hill, Theodore Roosevelt and his **Rough Riders,** a volunteer force of college students, cowboys, and adventurers, took the Hill with the heavy assistance of the Fourteenth Regiment Colored Calvary.

After the United States claimed victory in Cuba on July 1, it invaded the Spanish colony of Puerto Rico, where the exhausted Spanish signed a ceasefire with the United States in August 1898. The peace treaty was signed in Paris. Spain gave the United States the Pacific island of Guam and the Caribbean island of Puerto Rico. The most difficult decision was what to do with the Philippines. President McKinley was stuck. He could give the Philippines its promised independence and risk the possibility of a radical dictator or a European power seizing control of the islands, or he could take the islands and face the court of world opinion. He decided that the United States would take the Philippines and deal with the independence issue at a later date.

Repercussions of Expansionism

In the United States, the debate over expansionism intensified. Anti-imperialists such as **William Jennings Bryan** even formed an organization to oppose U.S. expansion publicly. Citizens living in newly conquered territories took cases involving their constitutional rights all the way to the U.S. Supreme Court. In its 1901 **Insular Cases** decision, the Court ruled that the Constitution and its protections did not follow the flag (meaning that a citizen in a conquered territory was not necessarily protected by the Constitution). It was up to Congress to decide the rights of the people in the newly conquered territories.

As Cuba got ready to draft its constitution, the United States began to waver on its Teller Amendment promise to give Cuba independence with no strings attached and issued the **Platt Amendment**, which Cubans would now have to write into their new constitution to gain freedom. The Platt Amendment specified that Cuba could only sign treaties after the United States had approved them, gave the United States the right to interfere politically and militarily in Cuban affairs, and allowed the United States access to naval bases on the island. This meant, in essence, that the Cubans had not gained their independence at all.

The Filipinos, led by a former American ally named Aguinaldo, revolted against the American presence. In 1899, this became horrible jungle guerrilla warfare between the Filipino revolutionaries and Americans. After Aguinaldo was captured in 1901, his fighters were subdued. The Philippines did not gain its independence until 1946.

China was of concern to American investors. Japan and Europe had already carved China into spheres of influence whose economic dealings they controlled. Hoping to get a piece of the action, Secretary of State John Hay issued his "**Open Door Policy**" in 1899. Under this plan, China and her surrounding regions would be free to trade with any nation. Wildly popular in the United States, the policy received a cold shoulder abroad. Then, a young group of Chinese nationalists revolted against the Open Door Policy and foreign intervention. The **Boxer Rebellion** of 1900 sought to remove forcibly all foreigners from China. After the rebels killed some 200 whites, a multinational force that included U.S. troops was sent to Peking to end the rebellion.

The Panama Canal

The canal that Mahan had suggested became more than an idea when Americans and Europeans sought to build it across the Isthmus of Panama. Ferdinand de Lesseps, who had built the Suez Canal, had begun the construction in 1882. Unfortunately, he lost workers to disease, and the tropical climate and geography gave rise to engineering problems. The United States wanted to take on the building of the canal, but several things stood in the way. It seemed doubtful that the Colombian government would grant permission to build the canal. Of course, if the canal did not cross Colombian territory, Colombia's consent would not be needed. The nation of Panama would have to be created, and quickly! Secretly, with the aid of the French, President Theodore Roosevelt raised a revolutionary force to fight for Panamanian independence from Colombia. The "revolution" ended as quickly as it began; Roosevelt immediately recognized the new nation. It came as no surprise that the Panamanian government granted the United

States exclusive rights to build the canal in 1903. Construction was completed in 1914. Roosevelt's critics branded his actions in Panama "**gunboat diplomacy**," and Latin American countries watched in alarm as the "**Colossus of the North**" flexed its muscles throughout the region.

The Roosevelt Corollary Changes Relations Abroad

LATIN AMERICA

President Roosevelt had his own style of imperialism. As Britain and Germany attempted to collect debts from Venezuela, he decided to protect the Latin American nation from European intervention, so he amended the Monroe Doctrine. His changes in U.S. policy, called the **Roosevelt Corollary**, stated that the United States would come to the aid of any Latin American nation experiencing financial trouble. The United States would now be Latin America's police officer. Under the new policy, the United States used force to "protect" the Dominican Republic and Cuba from political chaos.

U.S./JAPANESE RELATIONS

Roosevelt intervened in the Russo-Japanese War of 1904, when those nations feuded over regions of Korea and Manchuria. Because he did not want either nation to control the disputed regions, he approached Japan and offered to help it settle the war. After the **Treaty of Portsmouth** ended the conflict, Roosevelt won the Nobel Peace Prize for his role in mediating the treaty. As Japanese immigrants poured into San Francisco, white San Franciscans passed restrictive laws aimed at the incoming immigrants, outraging Japan. Roosevelt crafted a "Gentleman's Agreement" between the San Francisco School Board and the Japanese government, allowing Japanese students to enter public school if the Japanese government would help stem the tide of immigrants coming to California. To impress the Japanese and others with U.S. power, Roosevelt sent the U.S. Navy's mighty **Great White Fleet** around the world.

President Taft's "Dollar Diplomacy"

President Taft's foreign relations tactics were more economic than militaristic. Through **Dollar Diplomacy**, Wall Street investors sent their dollars to foreign countries, such as those in Latin America, to weaken their bonds with Europe and strengthen ties with the United States. However, Taft sent U.S. forces to invade Latin American countries in order to protect American interests on several occasions. These actions further alienated Latin America.

President Wilson's "Moral Diplomacy"

While President Wilson believed that imperialism was immoral, he also believed in the superiority of American democracy and thought it was his duty to spread that ideal to protect nations from totalitarianism. This policy became known as **Moral Diplomacy**. As a result, Wilson invaded Nicaragua and the Dominican Republic; purchased the Virgin Islands; and intervened in the Mexican Revolution, capturing the revolutionary **Pancho Villa** after he killed Americans in the towns of Santa Ysabel, Mexico, and Columbus, New Mexico. In 1917, the United States was finally forced to withdraw from Mexico's civil war. However, a dramatically larger war troubled President Wilson.

"The Great War" (World War I)

WWI BEGINS IN EUROPE, 1914

President Wilson wanted to keep the United States out of the affairs of Europe, but once a Serbian nationalist had assassinated the Archduke Ferdinand of Austria-Hungary in 1914, European military and political alliances, militarism, and extreme nationalism made European war inevitable. Events in Europe had devastating effects on the

American economy. After European nations demanded repayment of debt in gold and silver, the drain of hard specie produced a deep recession in the United States but by 1915, as the United States supplied Britain and France with munitions and foodstuffs, the economy improved.

U.S. neutrality was tested after both Britain and France imposed naval blockades against the Germans. The **German U-boats** (submarines) terrorized civilian and military shipping across the Atlantic. The Germans claimed that these ships might be carrying munitions for Britain or France and must be stopped. By September of 1915, German U-boats had sunk 90 ships in or near the Atlantic. When the British luxury liner *Lusitania* went down off the coast of Ireland in May 1915, almost 1,200 lives (about 130 of them American) were lost. President Wilson, who still did not want to enter the war, warned the Germans to stop attacking unarmed ships. When the Germans assaulted the French passenger liner *Sussex* in March 1916, killing four Americans, Wilson signaled America's willingness to go to war when he issued the **Sussex Ultimatum**, stating that the United States would break off diplomatic relations with Germany unless it ceased submarine warfare. Germany agreed to stop, if England lifted its blockade.

THE UNITED STATES ENTERS THE WAR, 1917

In January 1917, Germany announced that it would sink any ship violating the war zone, including American ships. Wilson immediately broke off relations with Germany. On March 2, 1917, Wilson learned that a British agent had intercepted and decoded a letter from the German foreign secretary Zimmermann to the German ambassador in Mexico. The message promised the Mexican president that if his country assisted Germany in a possible war against the United States, Mexico would gain the territory it had lost in the Mexican-American War after Germany won.

WILSON'S FOURTEEN POINTS

Wilson felt that it was his duty to **"make the world safe for democracy"** and enumerated how he planned to do this in his **Fourteen Points** speech to Congress on January 8, 1918. Wilson aimed to do away with secret treaties, free the seas, ensure economic freedom, reduce arms, end colonialism, and form an international organization for collective security.

THE COMMITTEE ON PUBLIC INFORMATION AND WAR INDUSTRIES BOARD

As the United States mobilized for war, the **Committee on Public Information** became a massive propaganda machine that urged Americans to buy war bonds and support the war effort. The **Food Administration** encouraged Americans to grow **"victory gardens"** and limit the amount of food they ate. Americans stopped using "German" names (frankfurters became liberty sausages), playing German music, or teaching German in schools. The **War Industries Board**, headed by Bernard Baruch, controlled American factory production, wages, and the prices of manufactured goods. As America's allies begged for men to fight the Germans, Wilson urged the passage of the **Selective Service Act (1917)**, which authorized the conscription of American men into service. Within months, the army had enough men to relieve the allied forces overseas.

WARTIME CURBS ON CIVIL LIBERTIES

Americans lost some civil liberties during the war, The **Espionage Act of 1917** and **Sedition Act of 1918**, which targeted Germans and antiwar protesters, curbed the right to free speech. Socialists like Eugene V. Debs were watched and arrested. In *Schenck v. United States* (1919), the Supreme Court upheld the Espionage Act by affirming that Congress could limit the right of free speech that represented a "clear and present danger" that would bring about "evils" that had to be stopped. The war years became an ugly time for civil liberties—many Americans were imprisoned into the 1920s and 1930s for wartime "crimes."

WILSON ATTENDS VERSAILLES PEACE CONFERENCE, 1919

On November 11, 1918, Germany signed an armistice with the Allied powers. The peace conference began on January 18, 1919, in the Palace of Versailles. The "**Big Four**" leaders—the United States' Wilson, France's Clemenceau, Italy's Vittorio Orlando, and Great Britain's David Lloyd George—were in attendance, and Germany and Russia were absent. Wilson wanted his Fourteen Point program written into the treaty, especially the part that called for the creation of a League of Nations, while the European leaders focused on exacting revenge from Germany. Wilson had to compromise. One area of compromise was the idea of "**mandates**," which put conquered territories under the trusteeship of the League. The Balkan and Baltic States were given independence, but Wilson got his League of Nations as well as Article X of the League's charter, requiring members to be available if another member nation's sovereignty was being threatened.

UNITED STATES DOES NOT RATIFY VERSAILLES TREATY OR ENTER LEAGUE OF NATIONS

The Republicans, who disliked Article X, were either **reservationists**, who would ratify if certain "reservations" were added to the League's Covenant, or **irreconcilables**, who refused to ratify. To save the treaty and the League of Nations, President Wilson traveled to bring his case to the people, but he collapsed in exhaustion in Colorado. Some days later, he suffered a stroke that left him partially paralyzed and unable to meet with his executive cabinet for seven months. The Senate twice voted not to ratify in 1919. The debate finally turned on whether the treaty would be accepted with reservations. While some Democrats voted with the reservationists, loyal Wilson supporters did not. Though Wilson hoped that the election of 1920 would be a "**solemn referendum**" by which Americans would give his Democratic Party continued control of the White House and a majority in Congress, the Republicans dominated the election. The United States did not officially end the war with Germany until 1921, and it never ratified the Treaty of Versailles or joined the League of Nations.

Postwar Problems at Home and Abroad

Many American veterans returned from Europe with missing limbs, facial disfigurements, and "**shell shock**" (now called posttraumatic stress disorder). The federal government did not have any plans for helping war veterans reestablish themselves in civilian life, and thousands of women and African Americans were let go so that war veterans could have jobs when they returned to the United States. As the country entered the 1920s, thoughts of Russia's 1917 **Communist Revolution** inspired fear at home. Americans worried that the **Bolsheviks**' pledge to destroy capitalism might bear fruit in the United States. After a series of bombings was attributed to anarchist groups, Attorney General A. Mitchell Palmer fanned the flames by ordering the roundup of all suspected anarchists, socialists, and aliens (usually Russian); 6,000 were arrested in 2 months, and 500 were deported. Layoffs and wage cuts after the 1919 recession had brought labor strikes and related violence. When this led many Americans to believe that communists had infiltrated the unions, the federal government began to look at strikes unfavorably. Massachusetts' governor, Calvin Coolidge, sent in the National Guard after Boston police officers struck for better wages and the right to organize. Racial issues also flared. After African American workers were fired so that returning war veterans could return to their former jobs, race riots broke out in Chicago, Baltimore, and Omaha as black Americans burned, looted, and raged against their conditions.

THINGS TO REMEMBER

PEOPLE

Freedmen's Bureau
scalawags
carpetbaggers
sharecroppers
Ku Klux Klan
Redeemers
Exodusters
Rutherford B. Hayes
George Custer
49ers
sodbusters
National Grange of Patrons
  of Husbandry
Interstate Commerce
  Commission
Cornelius Vanderbilt

Andrew Carnegie
John D. Rockefeller
Horatio Alger
robber barons
U.S. Steel
Standard Oil Company
scabs
National Labor Union
Knights of Labor
American Federation of
  Labor
Pullman Palace Car
  Company
"Boss" Tweed
Thomas Nast
Jane Addams

Francis Willard
Carrie A. Nation
Elizabeth Cady Stanton
Susan B. Anthony
Mark Twain
Frederick Law Olmsted
Scott Joplin
Joseph Pulitzer
William Randolph Hearst
Jacob Coxey
Theodore Roosevelt
Ida Tarbell
Lincoln Steffens
Jacob Riis
Robert La Follette
Samuel Gompers

Mother Jones
Carrie Chapman Catt
Booker T. Washington
W. E. B. Du Bois
Alice Paul
William Jennings Bryan
Archduke Francis
  Ferdinand
Rough Riders
Great White Fleet
Committee on Public
  Information
War Industries Board
Big Four
League of Nations
Socialists

EVENTS

Reconstruction
The Great Railroad Strike
The Gilded Age
Panic of 1893

"Cross of Gold" speech
Progressive Era
Wisconsin Experiment
Great Migration

Seward's Folly or
  Seward's Icebox
Spanish-American War
Boxer Rebellion

Gentlemen's Agreement
Great War
Communist Revolution
Red Scare

TERMS

Black Codes
sharecropping
pardons
filibuster
long drives
Ghost Dance
grandfather clauses
agribusiness
transcontinental railroad
vertical integration
horizontal integration
interlocking directorates
laissez-faire
nouveau riche
social Darwinism
trickle-down theory
yellow-dog contract
closed shops
scabs

depression
arbitration
collective bargaining
social gospel
ghettos
tenement
political machines
temperance
Nativists
Woman's Christian
  Temperance Union
Anti-Saloon League
National American Woman
  Suffrage Association
Stalwarts
Halfbreeds
Mugwumps
Greenback Party
Farmers' Alliance

Populist Party
Gold Bugs
muckrakers
Northern Securities
  Company
Federal Trade Commission
National American Women
  Suffrage Association
National Women's Party
Niagara Movement
League of Women Voters
National Association for
  the Advancement of
  Colored People (NAACP)
initiative, referendum,
  and recall
accommodation
spoils system
patronage

direct primaries
jingoism
reconcentrating
yellow journalism
gunboat diplomacy
Dollar Diplomacy
Moral Diplomacy
U-boat
Lusitania
mandates
reservationists
irreconcilables
imperialism
nationalism
spheres of influence
self-determination
reparations

THINGS TO REMEMBER

PLACES

Sutter's Mill	Union Pacific Railroad	Triangle Shirtwaist Factory	Versailles
Central Pacific Railroad	Promontory Point		

LAWS AND DOCUMENTS

Proclamation of Amnesty and Reconstruction	Homestead Act of 1862	Hepburn Act	Platt Amendment
	Plessy v. Ferguson	*The Jungle*	Open Door Policy
Wade-Davis Bill	Jim Crow laws	Pure Food and Drug Act	Hay-Pauncefote Treaty
10 Percent Plan	Interstate Commerce Act	Meat Inspection Act	Roosevelt Corollary
Civil Rights Bill of 1866	*A Century of Dishonor*	Mann-Elkins Act	Treaty of Portsmouth
Fourteenth Amendment	Sherman Antitrust Act	Sixteenth Amendment	Sussex Ultimatum
Military Reconstruction Act	*United States v. E. C. Knight*	Underwood Tariff Bill	Fourteen Points
Tenure of Office Act	Chinese Exclusion Act	Federal Reserve Act	Selective Services Act
Fifteenth Amendment	*Our Country*	Federal Reserve System	Espionage Act
Force Acts	Pendleton Civil Service Act of 1881	Clayton Antitrust Act	Sedition Act
The Compromise of 1877		Nineteenth Amendment	*Schenck v. United States*
Turner's Frontier Thesis	Seventeenth Amendment	*Birth of a Nation*	Article X
Dawes Severalty Act of 1887	Square Deal	Teller Amendment	
	Elkins Act	Insular Cases	

Practice Section

❯❯ DOCUMENT-BASED QUESTION

Suggested writing time: 45 minutes

The following question requires you to write a coherent essay incorporating your interpretation of the documents and your knowledge of the period specified. To earn a high score, you are required to cite key pieces of evidence from the documents, drawing on your knowledge of the period.

1. Using your knowledge of the periods 1830–1850 and 1880–1900 and Documents A–G, construct a coherent thesis that compares and contrasts antebellum and Progressive reform movements. Be sure to address the social, political, and economic impact of each movement in your answer.

Document A

Excerpt from the Declaration of Nicholas Fernandez, executed in Cadiz Harbor in 1829 for piracy and murder: "Parents into whose hands this, my dying declaration may fall, will perceive that I date the commencement of my departure from the paths of rectitude and virtue, from the moment when I become addicted to the habitual use of ardent spirits—and it is my sincere hope that if they value the happiness of their children—if they desire their welfare here, and their eternal well being hereafter, that they early teach them the fatal costs of Intemperance!"

Document B

William Lloyd Garrison, 1830: "Even the 'glorious gospel of the blessed God,' which brings life and immortality to perishing man, is as a sealed book to his understanding. Nor has his wretched condition been imposed upon him for any criminal offence. He has not been tried by the laws of his country. No one has stepped forth to vindicate his rights. He is made an abject slave, simply because God has given him a skin not colored like his master's; and Death, the great Liberator, alone can break his fetters!"

Document C

Angelina Emily Grimke, Letter XII (October 2, 1837), Letters to Catherine E. Beecher *(Boston: I. Knapp, 1838):* "The regulation of duty by the mere circumstance of sex, rather than by the fundamental principle of moral being, has led to all that multifarious train of evils flowing out of the anti-Christian doctrine of masculine and feminine virtues. By this doctrine, man has been converted into the warrior, and clothed with sternness . . . whilst woman has been taught to . . . sit as a dollar arrayed in "gold, and pearls, and costly array," to be admired for her personal charms, and caressed and humored like a spoiled child, or converted into a mere drudge to suit the convenience of her lord and master . . . ."

57

Document D

Brigham Young, 1854 letter to Thomas Kane: "In our Mountain home we feel not the withering sources of influence of political or even fashionable despotism. We breathe free air, drink from the cool mountain stream, and feel strong in the free exercise of outdoor life. I have traveled on several hundred miles this season among the native tribes, to conciliate their hostile feelings, and cause them to become friends. I have found the satisfaction of having been eminently successful; peace again smiles upon all our settlements, and that too without a resort to arms."

Document E

Eyewitness Account of the Triangle Shirtwaist Factory Fire, 1911: "I was upstairs in our work-room, when one of the employees who happened to be looking out of the window cried that there was a fire. I rushed downstairs, and when I reached the sidewalk the girls were already jumping from the windows. None of them moved after they struck the sidewalk. Several men ran up with a net which they got somewhere, and I seized one side of it to help them hold it. It was about ten feet square and we managed to catch about fifteen girls. I don't believe we saved over one or two however. The fall was so great that they bounced to the sidewalk after striking the net. Bodies were falling all around us, and two or three of the men with me were knocked down. Girls just leapt wildly out of the windows and turned over and over before reaching the sidewalk.

Document F

Jane Addams, 1885: "Teaching in a Settlement requires distinct methods, for it is true of people who have been allowed to remain undeveloped and whose facilities are inert and sterile, that they cannot take their learning heavily. It has to be diffused in a social atmosphere, information must be held in solution, in a medium of fellowship and good will. . . . It is needless to say that a Settlement is a protest against a restricted view of education."

Document G

The Volstead Act, 1919: "The term 'War Prohibition Act' used in this Act shall mean the provisions of any Act or Acts prohibiting the sale and manufacture of intoxicating liquors until the conclusion of the present war and thereafter until the termination of demobilization. . . . The words 'beer, wine, or other intoxicating malt or vinous liquors' in the War Prohibition Act shall be hereafter construed to mean any such beverages which contain one-half of 1 per centum or more of alcohol by volume."

❯❯ HOW TO APPROACH THE DOCUMENT-BASED QUESTION

As you approach this prompt, you should begin by "dissecting" the question. Underline directions and other words that give you clues as to the intent of the prompt. This prompt clearly asks the writer to consider two periods of reform and their social, political, and economic impact on the United States. It is important to note that the directions specify that you compare and contrast the time periods; use the documents and address the categories of the acronym PERSIA noted in chapter 1.

Now, before looking at the documents, formulate a thesis based solely on your own background knowledge. If this step gives you trouble, then you know you will not have much outside information to draw upon. Remember, outside information is *required* on the DBQ.

Next, do a quick brainstorm of the social, political, and economic factors you remember from the time periods mentioned. You may wish to create lists of terms and people under each heading to aid you in writing your body paragraphs. Your list may include some of the following: abolitionists, William Lloyd Garrison and *The Liberator,* the Grimke sisters, Women's Christian Temperance Movement, utopian societies, Mormons, Andrew Jackson, Second Great Awakening, Market Revolution, rise of industry, child labor laws, white lung, Prohibition, settlement house movement.

You now need to move to the documents. Quickly use the SCIT method of analysis:

Scan
Catalog
Infer
Tie it Together

By the time you take the AP exam, you should be able to complete SCIT for all of the documents in 10 minutes or less.

Finally, it is time to write your thesis. A possible answer may postulate that the antebellum and Progressive reform movements were very much alike in that they both involved middle-class whites trying to better society through influencing the government. You may also choose to say that the movements were very different in that the antebellum movements were more driven by religious beliefs and a need for perfectibility, while the Progressives were simply trying to protect themselves from massive social and economic change. Either way, you would need to make sure that you provide enough information from the documents and your own list to support your thesis.

❯❯ DBQ ANALYSES

Document A:

Inferences: These criminals acted due to their addiction to "ardent spirits," or alcohol. Mr. Fernandez is imploring those watching the execution to teach children to remain temperate and not consume alcohol. This document was widely used by the early temperance movement as evidence of the evils of drinking alcohol.

Document B:

Inferences: This excerpt was taken from Garrison's *The Liberator* in one of its earliest printings. It is clear that the author is a religious man and likens the liberation of slavery to a Christian moral duty. One may see the connection between this document and the Second Great Awakening.

Document C:

Inferences: Impacted by the Second Great Awakening and the abolitionist movement, the Grimke sisters soon took up the charge of women's rights. Angelina Grimke is writing this letter to fellow abolitionist and feminist Catherine Beecher bemoaning the state of the pampered woman. It is clear from this document that Grimke feels the new stature of women is far from "Christian."

Document D:

Inferences: One would have to know that Brigham Young was the second major leader of the Mormons and moved his people across the country to "Deseret," or Utah, to find their sacred homeland. Colonel Thomas Kane was a lifelong friend of the Mormons, fighting for political protections and even physical war for them. Late in his life, he converted to Mormonism. The Mormon movement can be viewed as an example of people searching for a utopia to practice their faith and lifestyle in peace, much like Oneida and Brook Farm.

Document E:

Inferences: One of the most deadly industrial fires in U.S. history occurred at the Triangle Shirtwaist Factory in 1911. Young girls and women were trapped inside the factory behind locked windows and fire escapes. Girls as young as 15 jumped from the high-rise windows to escape the fire and ultimately met their fate on the sidewalk below.

The 148 girls and women who perished in the fire sparked a wave of reform aimed at better working conditions and laws to limit the work hours of women.

Document F:

Inferences: Jane Addams was a new breed of Progressive in that she was one of a new stock of college-educated women. Taking her knowledge of life and society to Chicago, Addams opened Hull House as a way to provide a clean respite to the destitute of the city. She also offered courses in manners, decorum, and reading at the house to teach indigents how to succeed in society.

Document G:

Inferences: This document can be used with Document A to explain that the Temperance Movement had not disappeared by 1919. The Volstead Act was the legal arm of the Eighteenth Amendment, thus enforcing Prohibition. It was widely thought that alcohol was the root of all evil and to ban it would solve the country's problems with crime and poverty.

❯❯ SCORING GUIDE

Monitoring your own success on the exam's essay section is straightforward. The scoring guides for the DBQ and the FRQ are very similar. Essays on the AP U.S. History exam are all scored on a nine-point scale. Basic requirements hold true from year to year, with the content requirements changing for each question asked. A standard nine-point scoring guide would look something like this:

The 8–9 essay

- Contains a clear, well-developed thesis that answers all parts of the prompt.
- Thesis is supported with substantial, relevant information.
- Provides evidence of thoughtful analysis.
- May contain minor errors.

The 5–7 essay

- Contains a thesis that answers all parts of the prompt; may be unbalanced.
- Thesis is supported with some relevant information.
- Analysis is unbalanced and/or limited.
- May contain errors that do not seriously detract from the quality of the essay.

The 2–4 essay

- Contains a confused or unfocused thesis or may simply restate the question.
- Contains minimal or irrelevant information or simply lists facts with no explanation.
- Contains little or no evidence of analysis and only a general treatment of information.
- May contain substantial errors.

The 0–1 essay

- Lacks a thesis or rewrites the question.
- Incompetent or inappropriate response.
- Shows little or no understanding of the question.
- Contains major factual errors.

The "–" essay

- Is blank or off-topic.

Essays are scored holistically, with Faculty Consultants (Exam Readers) reviewing each essay from beginning to end. Only actual essays are scored, which means that even if you have a great outline of an essay, you will receive a score of "–" if you do not write the essay in full.

❯ SAMPLE STUDENT RESPONSE

Both the antebellum (1830–1850) and Progressive (1880–1920) reform movements worked hard to create a better society for people to live in. The two movements are similar in goals and impacts but differ in the methods they used to achieve their goals. Antebellum and Progressive movements were created to combat the vices existent in American life. The antebellum reform movements attempted to persuade people by appealing to their conscience, whereas Progressive reformers went straight to the government to achieve their objectives. Progressives also used muckraking to get the attention of the people and government. In terms of overall patterns, the antebellum reform movements sprang from the Great Awakening and had more to do with changing the United

States into a Christian ideal. Conversely, Progressive reforms were centered on the idea of creating a fair and perfect society for every American. Because of this, the antebellum reformers had a greater social impact on society, whereas the Progressive reformers had more of a political and economic influence. The antebellum and Progressive reforms had much in common in terms of objectives and overall impact. Both aimed to remedy society's ills, and they both achieved part of their goals by making the United States a better place to live. The two movements had similar campaigns, such as temperance and women's rights. Also, both the antebellum movement and Progressive movement were created as a response to the rise of cities and industry. In the cities were vice, in industry there was immoral practices, and corruption existed in American society, government, and economic system. Another similarity between the two movements is that both antebellum reformers and Progressives were from the middle class. The antebellum middle class wanted to save both the lower and upper classes from sin, whereas the Progressive middle class acted out because they were hurting from the big trusts existing above them, as well as the hordes of immigrants from below who worked for cheap prices. The movements were most similar to each other in terms of the objectives they shared, and the fact that both made impacts on aspects in the lives of American citizens.

The differences in methods of campaigning clearly separate the antebellum reformers from the Progressive reformers because the former used more social means to achieve their goals (hence, they had a greater social impact in the United States), whereas the latter used aggressive political, economic, and muckraking techniques (so their major influences were mostly in the political and economic area). The antebellum reform movements were created as a result of the Second Great Awakening, the second Christian revival to hit the United States. As a result, feelings of tolerance, equality, and compassion created the Abolitionist Movement, who fought against Garrison's description of an African American's life in Document B. Alcohol addiction, which caused the "departure from the paths of rectitude and virtue" (Document A), was another vice that Christians felt it was their duty to warn society about. The utopian movements where people set up communes in places where the evils of society could not touch them (Document D) were also started by groups who were looking to preserve certain moral and/or Christian values. The reform movement concerned with education was partially caused by the Christian goal to reduce violence in society; in this case, the means of which was education at a young age in order to steer the youth away from lives of crime. Dorothea Dix's work for better mental health treatment was motivated by the Christian teachings of love and compassion for other human beings, no matter how different they are. Even the women's rights movement of the antebellum era was working toward making the modern woman into a better Christian, rather than "a spoiled child" who is made "to suit the convenience of her lord and master . . ." (Document C).

Conversely, most of the Progressive movements were caused by a want to improve society for everyone. It was more concerned with human welfare than creating a Christian society. A similarity between the reform movements was in the crusade against alcohol, which continued until the passage of the Eighteenth Amendment. Many called the 18th Amendment a success of the Progressive movement; however, the noble experiment of prohibition failed and the amendment was finally repealed in 1933. The labor movements fought against the exploitation of men, women, and children workers through unfair wages, hours, and working conditions. Jane Addams' work in offering people shelter from the vices of the city helped by giving them a place to go where they could escape the harshness of city life (Document F). The muckraking about the meat industry helped by warning them about what they were putting into their bodies; and the environmental muckraking assisted the public by making them aware of how their world was being violated, showing them what they could do to stop it. The women's rights movement was a reform designed to give women more control over their lives. The war fought against trusts kept the consumers and producers from getting trampled on by big businesses. Though both Progressive reform movements and antebellum reform movements helped create a better, cleaner United States, there is a fine line of difference between them. The antebellum reform movements were motivated by a public desire to spread Christianity, while the Progressive reform movements were driven by the need to keep people from being taken advantage of, exploited, or made inferior.

Another contrast between the two reform movements was their plan of action. The antebellum reformers relied on the conscience of the public to enact change. They appealed to society to change their ways by using religious, moral, logical, and emotional arguments. For instance, a typical argument used against alcohol would be that it causes people to act violently and irresponsibly, which could result in harm to both the alcoholic and his loved ones. This technique would emotionally guilt-trip people into not drinking, because they did not want to be the reason for their family's demise. Because of their tactics, the antebellum reformers had a great social impact on the people, as they worked hard to change the point of view of American society as a whole. They used their Christian arguments to appeal to people's hearts, which is something the Progressives could not do, because their reforms were not based on Christianity.

In contrast, the Progressive reformers used the government and economy to accomplish their goals. Instead of appealing to the emotions and minds of society, the Progressives went straight to the government to get what they wanted. For example, after the Triangle Shirtwaist Factory Fire in 1911 (Document E), the Progressives were able to make political headway that included laws protecting both women and child laborers. Overall, the government actions the Progressives wrangled had more meaning and weight than the social support gained by the antebellum reformers. Though the prohibition laws didn't last, the groundwork made by the Progressives was clearly much more far-reaching than the work of the antebellum reformers. The Progressives' political successes (initiative, referendum, and recall) gave the American people a chance to play a larger role in the government. Their economic successes (through labor movement successes and Roosevelt's Progressive-inspired trust busting) enabled people to have more economic opportunity and helped them not to be exploited by powerful businesses. Because of the difference between the plan of action of antebellum reforms and Progressive reforms, the two groups also differed in their effectiveness. The antebellum movements were less aggressive, and appealed to the people, and consequently they had a big social impact on American society. However, the more aggressive political strategy of the Progressives earned political and economic successes which last longer and were more solid in the lives of the American people.

CHAPTER 4

Aftermath of World War I through World War II: 1919–1945

❯❯ THE 1920S AND A NEW ERA: 1919–1945

The United States After WWI

As the country entered the 1920s, Presidents Harding, Coolidge, and Hoover protected the nation's wealthy businesspeople and insulated them from litigation. The country had emerged from World War I as a creditor nation. Industrial production soared in response to the appetite for manufactured goods. Despite strikes and losses that labor endured in 1920 and 1921, workers' wages were higher than they ever had been. Amidst this prosperity, business owners were less amenable to unionized employees,

> ▶ **AP EXPERT TIP**
>
> If you're having a hard time keeping all the dates straight in your head, try making a timeline of significant events.

and union membership sank to an all-time low. While the average American enjoyed a standard of living that was higher than that in any other nation, the very poor lived very poorly. Farmers did not get good prices for their crops and were burdened by debt.

MANUFACTURING AND THE AUTOMOBILE

Frederick W. Taylor's principles of scientific management made factory production fast and efficient. By giving each employee one specialized task, **Henry Ford**'s **assembly line** factories turned out cars at a previously unthinkable rate. As mass production created a mass consumption society, Ford produced affordable automobiles. By 1929, 30 million cars were on the road. The car revolutionized American life. Industries that contributed to its manufacture boomed, while railways lost business. Suburbs grew because cars enabled residents to live outside cities while commuting to work in them, and the car changed courtship among the young. Electrically powered refrigerators, vacuum cleaners, stoves, and irons became part of the new standard of living. The credit industry boomed.

The Scandalous Presidency of Warren G. Harding (Republican), 1921–1923

Harding became president by promising Americans "**normalcy**." Progressivism gave way to a long era of isolationist Republican administrations that favored business and consumerism. A handsome, poker-playing man from Ohio, Harding surrounded himself with capable and powerful men. His cabinet, dubbed the **Ohio Gang** or the **Poker Cabinet**, was made of old friends who were specialists in the areas in which they served. Because a naval arms race among the United States, Britain, and Japan was brewing, his secretary of state organized the **Washington Disarmament Conference,** held in 1921 and 1922 to address security issues. The participating countries (Belgium, China, France, Portugal, Japan, Italy, the Netherlands, and the United States) signed several treaties that purported to limit arms buildup and enhance territorial respect among all present. The **Dawes Plan**, a 1924 program to loan money to Germany (so that Germany could pay war reparations to Britain and France, so that those nations would have money to repay war debts they owed the United States), operated successfully until 1929. Harding's administration was disgraced in 1923, when it came out that two of his pals had illegally leased government oil fields near **Teapot Dome**, Wyoming, in exchange for cash and cattle. Harding's administration eventually gained the reputation of being one of the worst in American history. President Harding died of pneumonia in August 1923 leaving his vice president, Calvin Coolidge, to take over.

The Calvin Coolidge Presidency (Republican), 1923–1928

Coolidge took the oath of office in his parents' farmhouse in Vermont and set out to practice the Republican ideal of limited government. Less than a year later, he was reelected. "**Silent Cal**" was a man of few words who did very little as president. Whereas Woodrow Wilson would put in 12- to 15-hour days, Coolidge would work for 4 hours. Aside from assisting big business through inaction, he is mainly known as a president who refused to pay World War I veterans their promised bonuses and twice vetoed the McNary-Haugen Bill, which would have assisted farmers who badly needed price supports. He did not seek re-election in 1928.

Cultural Currents in the 1920s

Often called the **Jazz Age** or the **Roaring Twenties**, the era from 1920 to 1929 spawned its own culture. Ragtime music moved from the Deep South into northern cities like Chicago and Philadelphia and evolved into **jazz,** the preferred music of young urbanites. In 1920, commercial radio went on the air. The **National Broadcasting Company (NBC)**, soon reached into 5 million homes across the country with comedy, drama, and sports. Through this, Americans developed a common cultural identity. "**Moving pictures**" also became wildly popular and more sophisticated as silent films gave way to "**talkies.**" **Hollywood**, the California-based entertainment capital, became the epitome of glamour. Others were alienated by the country's materialistic, mass-consumption society. Such "**Lost Generation**" authors as **F. Scott Fitzgerald** and **Gertrude Stein** decried money madness and conservatism. Visual artists **Georgia O'Keeffe** and **Thomas Hart Benton** painted realist or early surrealist works with American themes unspoiled by consumerism. From **Harlem**, New York City's African American hub, came the **Harlem Renaissance**, which nurtured such writers as **Countee Cullen**, **Langston Hughes**, and **Zora Neale Hurston;** artists **Sterling Brown** and **Augusta Savage;** and jazz musicians **Louis Armstrong** and **Duke Ellington,** as they drew on their African American roots to become celebrated American artists.

CONSERVATIVE BACKLASH

A cultural struggle between the fundamentalists, prohibitionists, and nativists on the conservative right and the modernist left was also going on in the 1920s. In 1925, Tennessee barred the teaching of the theory of evolution. **John Scopes**, a biology teacher backed by the **American Civil Liberties Union (ACLU)**, defied the state statute by teaching Darwin's theory. He was represented by **Clarence Darrow** against fundamentalist **William Jennings Bryan,** who presented the state's case. The "**Scopes Monkey Trial**" became a press spectacle. Scopes was found guilty. The conviction was later overturned.

Prohibition and Organized Crime

The **Eighteenth Amendment** and its companion **Volstead Act** outlawed drinking but could not prevent it. Every city had secret clubs called "**speakeasies,**" where a whispered password ("speak easy") got one in. President Harding even served alcohol in the White House. Small-time distillers brewed "**bathtub gin**" for local clients; then organized crime commandeered the bootleg industry. Chicago crime boss **Al Capone**'s alcohol network soon branched into prostitution, drugs, and illegal gambling. Many soon called for the repeal of the Eighteenth Amendment, as the "noble experiment" was not engendering respect for the law.

Fear of Immigrants and Racism in the 1920s

IMMIGRATION

European immigrants and African American migrants continued to pour into American cities. In response to the re-emergence of **nativist** feelings, Congress limited the number of European immigrants who could come in. The **Emergency Quota Act** of 1921 limited the allowable number of immigrants coming from each nation to 3 percent of the 1910 census count. The **Immigration Act** of 1924, directed at southern and eastern European and Asian immigrants, followed, with a limit of 2 percent of the 1890 census number.

After a Massachusetts robbery and murder, Italian anarchists Nicola Sacco and Bartolomeo Vanzetti were arrested, convicted, and sentenced to death on evidence that was contradictory and confused. Though many Americans came to their defense, they were executed in 1927 after multiple appeals.

African Americans in the 1920s

African Americans and women continued to fight for basic civil rights and equality. **Marcus Garvey,** a young Jamaican immigrant, formed the **United Negro Improvement Association** and eventually started a "**Back to Africa**" movement. The movement collapsed after Garvey was convicted of mail fraud and deported in 1927. The NAACP and African Americans such as W. E. B. DuBois continued to press for justice and equality. Lynchings increased in the South.

THE KU KLUX KLAN

The KKK re-emerged, targeting Jews, Catholics, communists, and blacks and reviving the terror tactics it had used during Reconstruction. Many Southern and Midwestern government officials and police were members. After its former Grand Dragon was convicted of murder in 1925, the Klan went underground again.

Women's Issues

Many middle-class women had time on their hands, while poor and minority women had to work outside of the home to make ends meet. In 1921, Margaret Sanger founded the American Birth Control League and encouraged young women to prevent unwanted pregnancy, poverty, and abuse.

❯❯ THE GREAT DEPRESSION AND THE NEW DEAL: 1929–1938

The Hoover Presidency (Republican), 1929–1933

Though Hoover promised conservatism, prosperity, and progress for the nation, economic disaster came eight months into his term. He believed that, through "**rugged individualism**," anyone could become a success if he or she worked hard enough. In 1928, at the end of Coolidge's term, the **Kellogg-Briand Pact**, which strengthened isolationism, had been signed. This unenforceable treaty declared offensive wars illegal throughout the world but did not prohibit defensive warfare or stipulate punishment for countries that disobeyed the pact. After the Japanese threatened Manchuria in 1931, Hoover did intervene in a modest way. The **Hoover-Stimson Doctrine of 1932** declared that the United States would not recognize territorial gains made by nations who violated the Kellogg-Briand Pact. Hoover also initiated the **Good Neighbor Policy** with Latin America by withdrawing American forces from the region.

BACKDROP TO THE DEPRESSION

From 1819 to 1907, the United States experienced economic crises (usually called "**Panics**") every 20 years or so. These depressions were usually short-lived and corresponded with the natural business cycle. In 1929, values on the New York Stock Exchange had reached an all-time high, with stocks selling for more than 16 times their actual worth. Enticed by this "**bull market,**" many ignored the signs of impending crisis and risked their life savings in the stock market.

THE STOCK MARKET CRASHES

On "**Black Tuesday,**" October 29, 1929, the "**bubble**" burst. A selling frenzy on Wall Street drove prices to the floor. Assets became worthless overnight. The signs of coming trouble *had* been there. Americans had spent themselves into debt **buying on margin** (purchasing stocks with loans). **Overspeculation** (gambling that the value of an asset would continue to rise) had driven stock prices sky-high. Big business' trust in **supply-side theory** (that the supply of a good naturally created its own demand) led to overproduction of manufactured goods. When buying dwindled, manufacturers laid workers off or cut wages to maintain profits. Farmers who had purchased equipment on credit to keep up with innovations in agriculture were driven further into debt. Banks had issued risky property loans, leading to defaults, foreclosures, and ultimately bank failures. When banks failed, customers lost the money that the bank had been "keeping" in checking and savings accounts. Republican laissez-faire policies through the 1920s had not helped. High tariffs hurt American farmers and elicited retaliatory tariffs from other nations, which hurt U.S. manufacturers. Heavy debt burdens, war reparations, and the suspension of programs to rebuild Europe drove countries such as Germany and Britain deeper into recession, with global economic depression just around the bend.

HOOVER'S HARMFUL OR INEFFECTIVE RESPONSE

Hoover believed that Europe was responsible for America's financial crisis, so he increased the tariff on imported goods to almost 50 percent (**Hawley-Smoot Tariff**) and called for a worldwide debt moratorium on loans and World War I reparations. Certain that private charity should help the needy, he refused to help ordinary Americans. In 1932, as Congress created the Reconstruction Finance Corporation (RFC) to assist railroads, banks, and municipalities, a **Bonus Army** of World War I veterans asking for early release of bonuses Congress had promised to pay them in 1945 arrived in Washington, D.C., and set up a camp around the Capitol. Joined by thousands of other veterans and their families, they marched around the Capitol building and the White House. When Congress rejected the **Bonus Bill**, the remaining veterans clashed with local police. Two marchers died. Hoover called in the Army, which used tear gas and tanks on the unarmed protesters and burned the encampment. Americans followed these events with horror. Makeshift camps of unemployed men, called "**Hoovervilles,**" sprang up in cities across the country. Hoover had done more than his Republican predecessors by encouraging states and cities to institute public works projects to stimulate the economy and to employ the jobless. However, his staunch conservatism prevented him from halting the Great Depression.

Presidency of Franklin Delano Roosevelt Begins (Democrat), 1933–1945

FDR (who was Theodore Roosevelt's cousin) had been stricken by polio in 1921 and was paralyzed from the waist down. It was the tenacity of his wife, **Eleanor Roosevelt**, who encouraged her husband and campaigned for him when he was ill, that kept him in government after that. FDR had made a name for himself in state politics and as governor of New York. The public responded to his promise of a New Deal by electing him as president overwhelmingly.

THE FIRST NEW DEAL, 1933–1935

Roosevelt had goals (the "**Three Rs:**" relief, recovery, and reform) but no plan of action. To start out, he appointed a group of economists, professors, and politicians (the **"Brain Trust"**) to advise him, and he convinced Congress to pass legislation that would revolutionize the role of the federal government. During the "**First Hundred Days**," Congress approved bills that repaired the banking system, established government works projects that employed the jobless, offered subsidies to farmers, and revitalized industry. Now known as the **First New Deal**, the period that ran from 1933 to 1935 began with a two-day closure of all financial institutions. On the third day (by authority of the **Emergency Banking Relief Act**), only solvent banks would reopen their doors, while the federal government would take over the assets of insolvent institutions. To inform Americans of this, the president talked to the nation by radio, the first of many weekly "**Fireside Chats**" to follow. The president also took the United States off of the gold standard and exchanged all the gold held by private banks and individuals for Treasury notes (dollar bills). The **Glass-Steagall Act** (1933) authorized the formation of the **Federal Deposit Insurance Corporation (FDIC),** which would protect banking deposits up to $5,000 per deposit. Several acts designed to assist the "**relief**" effort came into being, along with an "**alphabet soup**" of government agencies such as the **Public Works Administration (PWA)**, to employ thousands of Americans rebuilding the country's infrastructure; the **Civilian Conservation Corps (CCC)**, to employ college- and high school-aged males to reforest America; and the **Tennessee Valley Authority (TVA)**, to supply the impoverished Tennessee Valley with hydroelectric power. The Supreme Court ruled that several other agencies were unconstitutional.

LABOR AND THE NEW DEAL

The National Industrial Recovery Act (NIRA) regulated industry, setting maximum work hours, minimum wages, and price floors, and curbed overproduction and price gouging by setting production quotas and inventories. Section 7a of NIRA formally guaranteed organized labor the right to collectively bargain, bringing legal acceptance to unions. **The American Federation of Labor (AFL)** was made up of white skilled workers who were not interested in seeing the union extend its protection to other workers. The **Congress of Industrial Organizations (CIO),** which wished to extend membership to all workers, focused on unskilled laborers in America's steel, automobile, and mining industries. The **National Labor Relations Act of 1935**, also called **the Wagner Act**, strengthened Section 7a of NIRA. During the Second New Deal, the **Fair Labor Standards Act** (1938) established a federal minimum wage and maximum hours for interstate businesses and ended child labor. Some industries did not want to let unions in. To drive its point home to General Motors in Flint, Michigan, the CIO's Lewis organized a "**sit-down strike**" of assembly-line employees in 1937. After the government refused to intervene, the company reluctantly recognized the **United Auto Workers (UAW)**. The UAW did not fare as well at the Ford plant, however, where workers were driven away before they could strike. The steel industry was also slow to accept unions.

THE SECOND NEW DEAL

The Second New Deal, which ran from roughly 1935 to 1938, focused on relief and reform. New congressional acts further increased the federal government's role in the lives of Americans. Established in 1935, the **Works Progress Administration (WPA)** employed a variety of Americans to build bridges, refurbish parks, write plays, and paint murals. The **Social Security Act (SSA)**, also passed in 1935, guaranteed benefits for retirees (if the SSA had been receiving monthly payments from their pay) once they turned 65. Unfortunately, the law did not cover workers such as domestics, nannies, and janitors, who were largely African American.

SUPPORTERS AND OPPONENTS OF THE NEW DEAL

Democrats stood by their charismatic president. Organized labor and blacks supported FDR and the Democratic Party. FDR appointed more African Americans to cabinet positions than had any previous president. His "Black Cabinet" promoted the repeal of Jim Crow laws in the South and antilynching legislation. Unfortunately, FDR needed the support of Southern Democrats and could not sign the legislation. Southern Democrats disliked FDR's attitude on race and gender relations, and conservative Northern and Southern Democrats who disagreed with FDR's handling of the Great Depression became Republicans. Supporters felt that the New Deal had rescued millions of Americans from poverty, cleansed the capitalist system, and renewed the spirit of self-preservation, but FDR had critics inside and outside his party. Extremists on both ends of the political spectrum charged that the president was either not doing enough or doing too much. Calling the New Deal "socialism," Republicans joined conservative Democrats to form the **American Liberty League** and tried to unseat FDR in the 1936 presidential race.

FDR AND THE SUPREME COURT

FDR tried to reorganize the Supreme Court after it had killed two of his bills. The **Judicial Reorganization Bill** (1937) would let the president appoint one justice for every seated justice over 70 years old, which would have given him six new justices. His opponents dubbed the bill (which eventually died) a "**court-packing scheme.**" Roosevelt did eventually make nine appointments to the Supreme Court.

THE ROOSEVELT RECESSION

After reduced government spending adversely impacted the economy in 1937 and 1938, FDR reluctantly increased spending on public works projects and other programs, and the nation's investment and employment increased. However, unemployment never dipped below 16 percent until mobilization for World War II pulled the country out of depression.

British economist **John Maynard Keynes** had questioned the classical economic model of supply-side economics, arguing that *demand* decided an economy's health. Keynesian theory proposed that the government should spend money it did not have (deficit spending) rather than try to balance the budget and increase taxes on an overtaxed system. Increased government spending would "prime the pump" by spurring investment, which would create new jobs.

THE END OF THE NEW DEAL

After the "Roosevelt Recession" in 1937, problems such as high unemployment and poverty remained. The midterm elections of 1938 replaced some Roosevelt stalwarts with Republicans and moderate Democrats, ending the New Deal.

Women, Okies, and Minorities in the Depression

Many women were obliged to find ways to bring in enough money to feed, clothe, and house a family in the Depression. If they could find jobs, they worked.

In the Great Plains, a drought killed crops and turned topsoil into powdery dust that blew away in the winds. Lured by flyers promising jobs and a good life, Texas and Oklahoma farmers (**Okies**) fled the **Dust Bowl** for California, where they found few jobs and plenty of discrimination, abuse, and humiliation. Nonetheless, many settled in California's Central Valley region.

Racial minorities fared worse, because available jobs went to whites. States and cities did not assist blacks and whites equally either. FDR, who needed the South's white vote, tread cautiously. African Americans did find a friend in Eleanor Roosevelt, who promoted several New Deal programs that accepted African Americans. After **A. Philip Randolph** threatened to march on Washington, the **Fair Employment Practices Committee (FEPC)** was formed to find defense industry jobs for blacks. Several federal programs employed Native Americans and improved their communities. **The Indian Reorganization Act of 1934** repealed 1887's Dawes Act, returned federal reservation lands to the tribes, and helped them re-establish and preserve tribal culture. When incoming Okies displaced Mexican Americans in the Southwest, many chose to go to Mexico. Others, some of them citizens, were rounded up and dumped on the Mexican border because the United States did not think they deserved jobs that "native-born" Americans would take.

❯❯ WORLD WAR II: 1939–1945

Prewar Realities

As **Adolf Hitler** violated the Treaty of Versailles, Americans were overwhelmed by their own domestic problems and did not want to get involved in another world crisis. President Herbert Hoover had ushered in the 1930s with diplomatic evasions, and Americans wanted isolationism. At the 1933 **Montevideo Conference,** FDR pledged that the United States would be a "good neighbor" and never intervene in Latin America. FDR also wanted to rid the world of the high protective tariffs that had crippled world economies. He formally recognized the **Soviet Union** as a sovereign nation in 1933 and declared the Philippines independent in 1934. But eventually, he could not ignore the totalitarian regimes that had gained power in Europe and Japan during the 1920s and early 1930s. Germans saw Adolf Hitler as their savior, Italians found hope in the words of the **fascist** leader **Benito Mussolini** ("il Duce"), and Japan expected glory from a military dictatorship. From 1935 to 1937, the United States enacted several neutrality acts and watched as America's European and Asian allies tried to keep the dictators at bay. When Hitler and Mussolini used the **Spanish Civil War** (1936–1939) as a military testing ground, the United States stood by. However, FDR increased military spending and began to "**prime the pump**" for war in 1938. By 1940, when he knew that war was drawing closer, FDR pressured Congress to pass the Selective Service Act, which required all American males between the ages of 21 to 35 to register for military service.

Hitler and Mussolini Eye Europe

Mussolini and Hitler intended to take over all of Europe. Mussolini invaded Ethiopia in 1935; the League of Nations condemned his actions but did nothing. Hitler violated the Versailles Treaty by invading the demilitarized (**Rhineland**) region between France and Germany in 1936. In 1937, Japan invaded China and "accidentally" sank an American ship on the Yangtze River. European leaders did not know how to handle Hitler's increasingly aggressive demands. In 1938, after Germany claimed the **Sudetenland**, a strip of land along the Czechoslovakian border, British Prime Minister **Neville Chamberlain** and French President **Edouard Daladier** met with Hitler to negotiate a settlement over the disputed territory. They did not invite **Czechoslovakia**. At this **Munich Conference**, France and England created the policy of "**appeasement**" when they offered to permit Hitler to take the Sudetenland if he promised not to invade any other territories. Though Hitler accepted the offer, his vow was short-lived, and Germany invaded all of Czechoslovakia six months later, then set its sights on Poland. Soviet leader **Josef Stalin**, whose country had been invaded by way of Poland many times throughout history, wanted Poland to be a neutral "**buffer zone**" between Germany and Russia. The world was surprised to learn that Stalin and Hitler, who were sworn enemies, had signed a secret **nonaggression pact** (which freed Germany to invade the western half of Poland with no resistance, while the Soviets would take the eastern half) in 1939. The British and French promised to declare war on Germany if an invasion occurred. On September 1, 1939, Hitler's forces rolled into Poland, and **World War II** began. Still, the United States announced its neutrality through the **Neutrality Act** of 1939. It also authorized the sale of U.S. weapons (on a "**cash-and-carry**" basis only). England and France, the only countries that had the naval capability to transport munitions, would have to pay cash and transport their purchased munitions themselves. This would eliminate the economic problems that could come with lending money for war and keep U.S. merchant ships out of the war zone. As the German air force (the **Luftwaffe**) bombed England and **U-boats** in the Atlantic and English Channel threatened British ships, England's new prime minister, **Winston Churchill**, pleaded for U.S. assistance. In consequence, the two nations made the **destroyers-for-bases deal**, through which the United States gave England several older U.S. naval ships in return for the right to establish U.S. military installments on British-held Caribbean islands.

Roosevelt's Third Term

AN END TO ISOLATIONISM

In 1940, President Roosevelt broke George Washington's precedent and ran for a third term. When he won the election with 54 percent of the popular vote, he took the victory as a mandate to end U.S. isolationism and become more involved in the war. He still emphasized diplomacy over combat, but it was clear that America would join the battle if necessary. In his January 1940 address to Congress, the president proposed that a **Lend-Lease Act** replace the ongoing "cash-and-carry" program. The United States would lend war materials to England to aid in the protection of the "**Four Freedoms**": Freedom of Speech, Freedom of Religion, Freedom from Want, and Freedom from Fear. Roosevelt also stressed that the program would benefit the U.S. economy. FDR and Churchill also met secretly to discuss postwar aims and draw up the **Atlantic Charter**, which declared that free trade and the self-determination of peoples would be the cornerstones of a world freed of fascism.

PEARL HARBOR

As Hitler continued to move on Europe, taking Paris in June, and Japan was poised to take French Indochina, FDR cut off Japan's supply of American raw materials. Because Japan was an island nation with few natural resources and relied heavily on the import of oil, FDR hoped to persuade the Japanese to remove their troops from China and Indochina in exchange for his lifting the U.S. oil embargo. He sent Secretary of State Cordell Hull to settle with the Japanese government. In the middle of the negotiations, the new Japanese leader, General Hideki Tojo, backed out. Though Hull did not know it at the time, the general was planning to cripple the United States through a secret attack on the Pacific fleet.

In the early morning hours of **December 7, 1941**, Japanese aircraft bombed the entire U.S. Pacific Fleet at Pearl Harbor, Hawaii. The surprise attack killed 2,400 American sailors and wounded 1,200 more. Eight battleships, including the USS *Arizona,* were sunk or severely damaged. Ten other ships and almost 200 planes were also damaged or destroyed in the attack. The president immediately asked Congress to declare war on Japan, and Congress responded with nearly unanimous support. Three days later, Germany and Italy declared war on the United States.

WARTIME MOBILIZATION

The country's draft system had already been established, and when the United States declared war on Japan, the Selective Service System expanded to include all 18- to 65-year-old males. Also, 260,000 women enlisted as members of the **Women's Army Corp (WACs)**, **Women Appointed for Voluntary Emergency Service (WAVES)**, and **Women's Auxiliary Ferrying Squadron (WAFS)**. These women supported the war effort by flying supply missions, decoding encrypted messages, and repairing machines. By the war's end, almost 16 million men and women had contributed to the war effort in some capacity.

The **Office of War Mobilization** was charged with shifting the country into a wartime economy. U.S. manufacturers now split their time between producing domestic and wartime goods. Unemployment all but vanished, as Americans went to work to fuel the war machine.

The **Office of Price Administration** and the **Office of Economic Stabilization** kept the economy under control by setting price floors and ceilings, regulating the tax code, rationing to ensure a sufficient supply of goods for troops overseas, and enabling manufacturers to make war items. American families put their money into savings (which would later benefit the postwar economy). The country was willing to sacrifice to win the war. As the national debt rose, all Americans were required to pay federal income tax, and the custom of issuing paychecks with tax already withheld and paid to the government began. The government borrowed money by issuing war bonds, which citizens purchased. Labor strikes were discouraged.

The **Office of War Information (OWI)** produced radio shows, news reels, posters, and cartoons to keep Americans apprised of events overseas and encourage participation in the domestic war effort. Americans were bombarded with information and propaganda about the war. Women were specifically targeted by promotions, such as the one involving "**Rosie the Riveter,**" which brought about 5 million women into the wartime workforce. Female workers typically earned two-thirds of a male salary.

Minorities During Wartime

America's ethnic minorities experienced changes in their lives. African Americans flocked to the North and the Southwest to seek jobs in factories, and, as in World War I, race riots broke out. NAACP membership surged. Eleanor Roosevelt called for desegregation of the armed forces. The **bracero** program invited Mexican Americans to the United States as migrant farm laborers, and many stayed on. Tensions between East Coast sailors awaiting deployment in Los Angeles and Long Beach ports and young Mexican American men grew. The **Zoot Suit Riots** occurred in the summer of 1943 when sailors roamed the streets looking for Mexican American teens wearing flashy clothes and beat them up. A special commission headed by Earl Warren found that the sailors and police had caused the riots. Native Americans enlisted in the armed forces or worked in factories across the United States. **Navajo Code Talkers** translated U.S. code into their Native American language so that enemy forces could not decipher the content.

WARTIME TREATMENT OF THE JAPANESE

In response to War Department paranoia, President Roosevelt issued **Executive Order 9066**, which removed 100,000 Japanese American citizens from their homes and sent them to internment camps. As a result, these Japanese Americans lost millions of dollars in potential income, property, and land. The Supreme Court upheld the decision to intern the Japanese in the case *Korematsu v. United States* (1944), stating that the curbing of civil rights was justified in wartime and that the Court could not second-guess military decisions.

The Big Three

By the time the United States entered the war, Hitler had invaded Russia through Poland. In an act of desperation, the Soviet Union joined the Allies. Roosevelt, Churchill, and Stalin, soon known as the "**Big Three,**" agreed to focus on getting rid of Hitler before dealing with Japan. Throughout the war, the Big Three met to discuss wartime concerns and postwar desires. Meetings yielded agreements and concessions that shaped the course of the war (and the later Cold War). In 1943, Roosevelt and Churchill met in **Casablanca** and decided to invade Sicily and demand "unconditional surrender" from the Axis powers. In November of 1943, all three met in **Tehran** to sow the seeds of the D-Day invasion. Stalin agreed to enter the war against Japan. The first disagreements between the Soviet leader and Churchill emerged when Stalin demanded Eastern Europe as a buffer between his country and Germany, while Churchill demanded a free Europe and a unified Germany after the war's end. Roosevelt mediated by promising peace through the proposed United Nations. At **Yalta** in February 1945, the three finalized plans for postwar Europe. Stalin agreed to enter the war against Japan within three months of Germany's surrender and signed an agreement to create a free and liberated Eastern Europe with free elections. Additionally, the Yalta conference yielded a blueprint for the United Nations and for dividing Germany into four occupied military zones. The final conference, the **Potsdam Conference,** took place after FDR's death.

The War against Germany and Italy

In the European "**theater,**" the Allies concentrated on eliminating **German U-boats** on the seas and the **German Luftwaffe** in the skies. **Radar**, a new British invention, enabled the **Royal Air Force** to shoot down German planes and the U.S. Navy to sink U-boats, which turned the tide of war against the Germans. In the south, the Allies struggled to rout the Germans, led by tank commander General **Erwin Rommel** ("the **Desert Fox**"), from the North African theater. In Tunisia, **Operation Torch,** under the command of U.S. General **Eisenhower** and British General **Montgomery,** put Rommel out of business in May of 1943. The Allies crossed the Mediterranean Sea and invaded the island of Sicily in September of 1943. In spite of fierce Italian and German resistance, the United States took the island in May of 1945. It was now time to liberate France. **Operation Overlord**, now known as the **D-Day** invasion, was an amphibious landing on **Normandy**'s beaches. Planned in utter secrecy, it could only succeed if it was launched in favorable weather. The opening arose on June 6, 1944, when a multinational force stormed the coast of Normandy. Although the cost in Allied lives was huge, the invasion proved a success and enabled the Allies to push onwards to liberate Paris by the end of August. The Allies then pushed into Belgium. In December of 1944 at the **Battle of the Bulge**, the Germans mounted a strong defensive attack. Though the Allies suffered losses in that battle, they were able to recover and keep pushing towards Germany. As British and U.S. air forces continued bombing, making German defeat imminent, Hitler took his own life (April 1945). On May 7, 1945, **V-E Day** (**Victory in Europe Day**), the Nazis surrendered. As Allied troops marched further into Nazi-held territory, they discovered massive **concentration camps** throughout Germany, Poland, Austria, and Czechoslovakia where Hitler had carried out the "**Final Solution**," his **genocide** of Jews and other ethnic groups.

Combating Japan

Early in the Pacific war, two naval battles served as turning points for the Allies. In the **Battle of the Coral Sea** (May 1942) and the **Battle of Midway** (June 1942), the Allies were able to prevent a Japanese aircraft carrier from reaching Australia. By breaking the Japanese communications code, the allies were able to intercept and destroy four more aircraft carriers. U.S. Admiral **Chester Nimitz** also adopted a strategy called "**island hopping**." The U.S. Navy advanced towards Japan via strategic Pacific islands and surrounded Japanese-held islands to engage the enemy. Eventually, this tactic would lead the Allies to the southernmost Japanese islands. The Japanese were not about to back down, however, and other bloody battles raged between 1943 and 1945. After V-E Day, the Allies turned all their attention to the Pacific Front and the Japanese, whose influence ranged from China and Indochina to the Korean peninsula, the Philippines, Indonesia, and many Pacific islands. The Allies had to rely heavily on naval supremacy and destroy the Japanese air force to win the war in the Pacific. By 1945, the United States had come close enough to the Japanese mainland to launch air raids on major cities. As the Japanese grew more desperate, however, they sent out suicide bombers called **kamikazes** to crash their planes into U.S. aircraft carriers.

President Harry S. Truman (Democrat), 1945–1953

Exhausted after the Yalta Conference, FDR was resting at his vacation home in Georgia when he died on April 12, 1945. A shocked nation learned that Harry S. Truman was now president. Truman attended the last of the Big Three Conferences, the **Potsdam Conference**, in July. The British had elected a new prime minister, Clement Attlee. The conference was contentious—all three men disagreed on just about every issue. It was evident that this group was on the brink of a breakup. However, the three leaders decided to demand an unconditional surrender from Japan, hold war-crimes tribunals after the war, and organize the occupation of Germany.

When Truman became president, America needed to win the Pacific war. Instead of invading Japan at the cost of many thousands of American lives, Truman decided to use a new secret weapon instead. On August 6, 1945, a few days after the Potsdam Conference, an atomic bomb known as "**Little Boy**" was dropped from the aircraft *Enola Gay* onto the industrial city of **Hiroshima.** It killed 80,000 people instantly, but the Japanese still refused to surrender without conditions. On August 9, a second bomb, "**Fat Man,**" was dropped on the island of **Nagasaki,** causing the immediate death of another 60,000 people. Japan surrendered on September 2, 1945.

Costs and Consequences of the War

The United States had suffered 800,000 casualties, spent $360 billion, and run up a staggering budget deficit. The United Nations was established to combat aggressive nationalism and to help countries in danger of invasion. Congress passed the **Servicemen's Readjustment Act** (the **GI Bill**), which funded college educations and provided low-interest home and small business loans to help servicemen transition back into civilian life. The birth rate soared. African Americans were given increased opportunities, and President Truman ended segregation in the federal government and armed forces. The Employment Act of 1946 aimed for 0 percent unemployment. The end of rationing and price regulations brought inflation. Republicans, who had not liked FDR's long presidency, limited the presidency to two terms via **The Twenty-Second Amendment**. The Republican Congress passed the **Taft-Hartley Act** (1947), which reduced the gains labor had made under Roosevelt. As families moved from the Rust Belt to the Sun Belt, Northern and Midwestern states were left with decreased tax revenues and sagging economies. Wartime technology gave way to consumer industries, while the public worried that nuclear weapons might fall into the hands of enemy states.

THINGS TO REMEMBER

PEOPLE

Frederick W. Taylor	Franklin Delano Roosevelt	United Auto Workers	Benito Mussolini
Henry Ford	Reconstruction Finance	Black Cabinet	Rosie the Riveter
William Jennings Bryan	Corporation	American Liberty League	Roosevelt
Sigmund Freud	Bonus Army	Okies	Churchill
John Scopes	Brain Trust	Fair Employment	Stalin
Dr. Francis Townsend	Congress of Industrial	Practices Committee	Luftwaffe
Huey P. "Kingfish" Long	Organizations	Il Duce	

EVENTS

Washington Disarmament	Black Tuesday	Second New Deal	Battle of the Bulge
Conference	First Hundred Days	Roosevelt Recession	V-E Day
Jazz Age	New Deal	Montevideo Conference	Zoot Suit Riots
Roaring Twenties	Gentlemen's Agreement	D-Day	

TERMS

scientific management	bull market	Women's Army Corps	Office of War Information
rugged individualism	Three Rs	Women Appointed for	Navajo code talkers
laissez-faire	Fireside chats	Voluntary Emergency	United Nations
speakeasies	margin	Service	appeasement
Poker Cabinet	repatriation	Women's Auxiliary Ferrying	cash-and-carry
Lost Generation	mobilization	Squadron	Four Freedoms
United Negro Improvement	anti-Semitic	Office of War Mobilization	bracero
Association	fascist	Office of Price	genocide
flappers	kamikazes	Administration	

PLACES

Dust Bowl	Sudetenland	Pearl Harbor

THINGS TO REMEMBER

DOCUMENTS AND LAWS

Dawes Plan
McNary-Haugen Bill
Kellogg-Briand Pack
Hoover-Stimson Doctrine
Good Neighbor Policy
Volstead Act
Quota Act
Immigration Act
National Origins Act
Hawley-Smoot Tariff

Emergency Banking Relief
Glass-Steagall Act
Public Works
    Administration
Civilian Conservation
    Corps
Tennessee Valley Authority
National Recovery
    Administration
Section 7a

Works Progress
    Administration
Social Security Act
National Industrial
    Recovery Administration
National Labor Relations
    Act
Fair Labor Standards Act
Judicial Reorganization Bill
Indian Reorganization Act

Selective Service Act
Neutrality Act of 1939
Destroyers-for-Bases
Lend-Lease Act
Atlantic Charter
Executive Order 9066
GI Bill
Employment Act of 1946
Taft-Hartley Act

Practice Section

1. The Emergency Quota Act of 1921

   (A) restricted the number of blacks in communities.
   (B) limited the number of European immigrants who could come into the United States.
   (C) was scorned by nativists.
   (D) was vetoed by the president.
   (E) garnered support from the Native Americans.

2. Which of the following did NOT contribute to the 1929 stock market crash?

   (A) Overspeculation
   (B) Purchasing stocks with loans
   (C) Trust in supply-side theory
   (D) Underproduction of goods
   (E) Overspending in the military

3. FDR's First Hundred Days are known as a period of time when

   (A) the Second New Deal replaced the First New Deal.
   (B) an enormous amount of innovative legislation was passed.
   (C) the administration did not permit banks to close.
   (D) the administration watched and waited while formulating its plan of action.
   (E) the government was in a state of chaos.

4. When FDR was re-elected for a third term, he took it as a mandate to

   (A) end U.S. isolationism.
   (B) strengthen the New Deal.
   (C) stand up to the Southern Democrats.
   (D) meet with leaders of all European nations, including Germany and Italy.
   (E) raise taxes.

5. The Lend-Lease Act was put in effect to replace

   (A) the cash-and-carry program.
   (B) other funding for the U.S. military.
   (C) the Four Freedoms programs.
   (D) Destroyers for Bases.
   (E) big-business agriculture with smaller family farms.

6. The New Deal ended because

   (A) the nation had surmounted the difficulties requiring New Deal legislation.
   (B) FDR lost congressional allies in the 1938 midterm elections.
   (C) it had only been meant to last for a few years.
   (D) it was unconstitutional.
   (E) the government ran out of money to fund it.

7. John Maynard Keynes

   (A) was a British economist who railed against deficit spending.
   (B) spoke out for supply-side economics.
   (C) strongly believed in balancing budgets.
   (D) believed that government spending was good for the economy.
   (E) supported immigration reform.

8. Radar was

   (A) a German technological breakthrough.
   (B) of little consequence until the last battles of the war.
   (C) developed too late to be of much use at sea.
   (D) crucial to the Allies' success.
   (E) created in the 1800s but not put to efficient use until WWII.

9. Roosevelt ordered Japanese American citizens sent to internment camps because of

   (A) his War Department's urging.
   (B) letters sent to him by citizens.
   (C) public opinion polls.
   (D) congressional requests.
   (E) his fear of the spread of communism.

10. The D-Day invasion

    (A) was planned in utter secrecy and had to be launched in favorable weather.
    (B) was carried out entirely by soldiers parachuted onto the battleground.
    (C) was so successful that few participants lost their lives.
    (D) was a relatively small, though successful, operation.
    (E) failed miserably.

Answers and Explanations

1. B

The Emergency Quota Act of 1921, which restricted the number of European immigrants who could come into the United States each year, reflected public and nativist sentiment. Fear of immigrants and racism were widespread, and this legislation acted on those feelings.

2. D

Many goods were overproduced, not underproduced, in the years leading up to the Great Depression. Manufacturers who relied on the supply-side notion that people would buy as much as factories could spit out found themselves with an oversupply of products they had paid to produce and could not sell. As a result, many of them had to lay off workers.

3. B

During FDR's "First Hundred Days," which began the period of his First New Deal, an unprecedented amount of legislation, which would revolutionize the role of the federal government, was passed. One of the first things he did was to order all banks to close for two days. On the third day, only those that were solvent reopened. The president and his advisors did not wait to act but did as much as they could as quickly as they could to change the country's direction.

4. A

When FDR was re-elected for a third term, he no longer enjoyed the congressional support that had enabled him to create and expand the New Deal, and war had overtaken Europe. Roosevelt took his re-election as a mandate to end U.S. isolationism and focus on foreign affairs. Though he did not want to go to war, he began to make the country ready for war if circumstances made it necessary.

5. A

The Lend-Lease Act was put in effect to replace the cash-and-carry program, through which the United States had been selling military and other supplies to European allies on condition that they pay cash for them and carry them away on their own vessels. Through Lend Lease, the United States would lend the Allies war materials to aid them in protecting the Four Freedoms (of speech, of religion, from want, and from fear).

6. B

The New Deal consisted of a series of legislative solutions to ongoing problems. When many of Roosevelt's congressional allies were replaced by Republicans and moderate Democrats in the 1938 midterm elections, he no longer had the votes necessary to push new programs through. This effectively ended the New Deal.

7. D

John Maynard Keynes was a British economist who did not accept classical supply-side economics. Keynes felt that that *demand* was more important to the economy's health and that deficit spending could be more beneficial than balancing the budget. He advocated increasing government spending to spur investment, which would then create new jobs.

8. D

Radar was a British invention that helped turn the tide of the war in the Allies' favor. It enabled the British to spot and shoot down German planes and was of similar help to the U.S. Navy, which used it to find and destroy German U-boats. Without this technology, the Allies would have been on shakier ground.

9. A

At the request of the War Department, President Roosevelt issued Executive Order 9066, which removed 100,000 Japanese American citizens from their homes and sent them to camps. The paranoia behind the request was later mirrored by the Supreme Court, which upheld the internment decision on the grounds that civil rights could be justifiably withheld in wartime.

10. A

The D-Day invasion was an enormous operation that had to be planned in utter secrecy and launched in favorable weather. A multinational force arrived on the beaches of Normandy; it travelled by air at night followed by amphibious landings by day. Despite an enormous number of casualties, the operation's goal was realized when those troops pushed in and soon liberated France.

CHAPTER 5

The Aftermath of World War II and the 21st Century

❯❯ THE COLD WAR: 1945–1963

With Secretary of State George Marshall, Undersecretary of State Dean Acheson, and Soviet expert George Kennan, President Truman set out to stop ("contain") communism from spreading. In so doing, he broke a tradition dating from Washington's Farewell Address by joining an alliance with European countries.

The Postwar Reality of the Soviet Union

The West soon came to distrust Joseph Stalin, as it became clear that he would not keep the promise to uphold the self-determination of Eastern European countries that he had made at Yalta. On the contrary, he prevented free elections and installed communist leaders in those countries, then turned them into **satellite** nations. Instead of preparing East Germany to rejoin West Germany as one sovereign nation of Germany, he turned East Germany into a communist state. In a speech in 1946, Winston Churchill declared, "An **iron curtain** has descended across Europe," referring to the grip of communism in Eastern Europe.

> ▶ **AP EXPERT TIP**
>
> When reviewing your notes and books for your regular tests during the school year, highlight those areas in your notes that you think you have forgotten (or never fully understood). That way, when the AP exam rolls around, you'll be able to revisit those notes and shore up your weak spots.

THE TRUMAN DOCTRINE, 1947

President Truman devised a plan to deal with Russia's ambitions through **containment**, a long-term strategy aimed at preventing the spread of communism into vulnerable countries by providing them with the aid they needed in order to become self-determining nations again. This was implemented through a number of programs, including the Marshall Plan and the National Security Act.

The **Marshall Plan** (1947) was a massive assistance plan, formed by Secretary of State George Marshall. It provided financial aid over four years to European countries willing to go the democratic route. It was also offered to the Soviet Union and other Eastern European countries, which refused the assistance. In Western Europe, the Marshall Plan was hugely successful.

The **National Security Act** (1947) replaced the old War Department and created the **Department of Defense**, the **Central Intelligence Agency**, and the **National Security Council**. A permanent peacetime draft was also enacted in 1948. **National Security Council Document NSC-68**, released in 1950 just after China fell to communism and the Korean crisis was about to begin, widened the scope of containment by authorizing the use of military aid.

THE BERLIN AIRLIFT, 1948

Stalin was adverse to any capitalist economic systems and had grown tired of U.S. involvement in European affairs. In 1948, Western powers sought to create a stabilized currency for the western sector of Germany. Stalin sent his troops to blockade all land routes into and out of Berlin. In response, Truman instituted the Berlin Airlift, which delivered supplies to the city every day for 11 months. Finally, Stalin reopened the city.

THE ARMS RACE, 1949

Soviet and Western alliances created an atmosphere in which each side attempted to beat the other by building up arms and superior large-scale weapons. After the Soviets developed and exploded their first atomic bomb in 1949, the atomic race was on. By 1952, the United States had developed and tested its first hydrogen bomb, which was at least one thousand times stronger than the bombs dropped on Hiroshima and Nagasaki.

Japan

Postwar Japan was occupied by the United States until 1951. America provided economic and political support and created a democracy. The Japanese constitution, written with the assistance of **General Douglas MacArthur**, retained a ceremonial emperor and a limited military.

China

The corrupt **Nationalist (Kuomintang)** regime under **Chiang Kai-Shek** (which the United States had kept in office during World War II) went to war with, and then fell to, **Mao Tse-Tung** and communist rule in 1949. The nationalists fled the mainland to **Formosa** Island (**Taiwan**). In 1950, Mao allied China with Stalin's Soviet Union.

Korea

Once a Japanese colony, Korea had been occupied by the Allies during World War II, when the Soviet Union held the north and the United States held the south. The Soviets then withdrew from the north part of peninsula, leaving it in the hands of its communist ally, **Kim Il Sung**. The United States left the south in the hands of **Syngman Ree**. Later problems erupted into the conflict called the Korean War.

❯❯ A SPLIT AMERICA: 1950–1959

The Korean Conflict, 1950–1951

With Communist Bloc aid, North Korea invaded South Korea at the **38th parallel**. President Truman reacted by urging the U.N. Security Council to intervene on behalf of South Korea. The Security Council authorized a military "**police action**" to liberate South Korea. The United States did *not* declare war. North Korea's army pushed into the South but U.S. General MacArthur's forces pushed it back towards the Chinese border. Chinese forces crossed the border and forced MacArthur back to South Korea. MacArthur wanted more resources; he ignored Truman's orders to conduct a "limited war" and demanded North Korea's unconditional surrender. Irate at MacArthur's insubordination, Truman fired him and called him home to make it clear that, in the United States, civilian rule was supreme. The conflict with North Korea ended in a stalemate, with both sides back at their original boundaries.

The "Red Scare" in the United States

Republicans felt that two Asian nations had been "lost" to communism and that Democrats were not acting to rid the world of the "**Red Menace**." Communist takeover paranoia swept the nation in the 1950s. Antisubversive congressional acts that had been drawn up around 1939 and 1940 were put into use. **The Smith Act**, which called for arresting people who advocated overthrowing the government, even if they did not plan to do so themselves, and the **House Un-American Activities Committee**, were both reactivated. Drawing upon actual cases in which Americans had been accused of leaking secrets to the Soviets, a couple named **Ethel and Julius Rosenberg** were prosecuted in a trial that became a press spectacle, convicted of treason and espionage, and put to death in the electric chair. After this, **Senator Joseph McCarthy** whipped the nation into an anticommunist frenzy, accusing (often falsely) many prominent people of communist connections. **McCarthyism** gained momentum, but the senator finally painted himself into a corner when his ruthless tactics during Senate committee hearings were shown on television.

Dwight D. Eisenhower Presidency (Republican), 1953–1961

A Republican administration, with war hero Dwight D. Eisenhower as president and anticommunist crusader Richard Nixon as vice president, was elected.

FOREIGN POLICY

The new secretary of state, **John Foster Dulles**, turned away from Truman's Cold War policies to practice "**brinksmanship**" (pushing an adversary to the brink of nuclear war and forcing it to back down in the face of U.S. superiority). In addition to brinksmanship, Dulles used covert action to push his Cold War agenda. In 1953, a CIA coup returned the corrupt **Shah of Iran** to power. In 1954, the CIA aided defeat of a liberal regime in Guatemala.

After the French were ousted from their last Indochinese colony in 1954, the **Geneva Convention** divided the region into three nations: **Cambodia, Laos**, and **Vietnam**. Vietnam was divided at the **17th parallel** in 1954, on the condition that elections to reunite the parts would occur two years later. **North Vietnam** had communist rule under **Ho Chi Minh**. **South Vietnam** had anticommunist rule led by **Ngo Dinh Diem**. Fearing that one nation's fall to the communists would trigger a sequence of similar events (the **Domino Theory**), Eisenhower prompted Dulles to create a NATO-like organization called **SEATO (Southeast Asia Treaty Organization)** to provide military aid to Diem's crumbling regime.

When Egyptian leader **Gamal Abdel Nasser** asked for U.S. assistance in building the Aswan Dam in his country, Eisenhower turned him down because he felt that Egypt was threatening Israel's security. In 1956, Nasser responded to the rebuke by seizing the **Suez Canal**, through which oil was transported from the Middle East to Europe and the United States. Without consulting Eisenhower, Britain, France, and Israel attacked Egypt and regained control of the canal. Eisenhower asked the UN Security Council to denounce the action and immediately remove the controlling forces. As the Truman Doctrine had done in regard to Europe, the **Eisenhower Doctrine**, which said that a country could request U.S. assistance if it were threatened by another country, made the United States a presence in a region—in this case, the Middle East.

U.S./Soviet relations were impacted when Stalin died in 1953 and was succeeded by **Nikita Khrushchev. The Warsaw Pact (1955)** was an alliance under which the Soviet Union provided military protection to satellite countries, with the condition that they could never leave the Pact.

After Hungary overthrew its Soviet puppet government and asked to leave the Pact, the **Hungarian Revolution of 1956** was brutally crushed by invading Soviet troops. Believing that U.S. intervention would bring about World War III, Eisenhower did not come to Hungary's aid.

In 1958, Khrushchev planned to expel all Westerners from Berlin but agreed to hold off pending a meeting with Eisenhower in Paris in 1960. Two weeks before the Paris talks, it was learned that the United States had been flying spy plans over the USSR since 1955. (This discovery was called the **U2 Incident**.) Khrushchev called off scheduled Paris talks with Eisenhower.

After overthrowing Cuba's brutal dictator, Batista, **Fidel Castro** nationalized lucrative American-owned businesses on the island. Eisenhower cut off relations with Castro, who turned to the Soviets, building a communist state. Eisenhower approved plans to invade Cuba.

DOMESTIC AFFAIRS AND COLD WAR FEARS

The National Highway Act of 1956, which created the nation's freeway system, did so (in part) so the nation could have it on hand for quick evacuation of urban centers and use it as emergency landing strips and for missile transport. In 1958, soon after the Soviet's 1957 launch of the **Sputnik** satellite, Congress created the National Aeronautics and Space Administration (**NASA**). Eisenhower warned of the dangers of letting the Cold War political machine (the "**military-industrial complex**") drive policy.

The State of Civil Rights in the 50s

The armed forces had been desegregated in the late 40s and **Jackie Robinson** became a pioneer as the first black in major league baseball in 1947. In 1954, the case of *Brown v. the Topeka Board of Education* reached the Supreme Court. NAACP lawyer **Thurgood Marshall**, who represented the Brown family, argued that their daughter should have the right to attend the same nearby neighborhood schools as did white children. The **Warren Court**'s decision that "separate facilities were inherently unequal" and had no place in public education effectively overturned *Plessy v. Ferguson*. Racial tension came to a head in 1957, when Arkansas governor **Orval Faubus** sent the National Guard to prevent nine black students, the "**Little Rock Nine**," from entering Little Rock's **Central High School**. A federal court ordered that they be admitted; violent protests broke out, and President Eisenhower called in federal troops.

On December 11, 1955, **Rosa Parks**, an NAACP secretary, made headlines when she was arrested in Montgomery, Alabama, for refusing to give up her bus seat to a white patron. **Dr. Martin Luther King Jr.**, a young minister from Georgia, organized blacks to boycott the buses, which were used almost entirely by blacks. Throughout the 400-day **boycott,** the black community organized car pools to transport hundreds of people to school, work, and home. When the Warren Court ruled that segregation on public buses was unconstitutional, the boycott ended. Dr. King and the **Southern Christian Leadership Conference (SCLC)** continued to challenge Jim Crow laws in Alabama and other Southern cities. Sit-ins grew to involve thousands, and students became the torchbearers for Dr. King, as the **Student Nonviolent Coordinating Committee (SNCC or "Snick")** was formed to keep the movement alive among the nation's young population.

President Eisenhower signed two modest civil rights bills. The **Civil Rights Bill of 1957** created a new division within the federal Justice Department to monitor civil rights abuses, and the **Civil Rights Act of 1960** extended the life of the Civil Rights Commission and gave the U.S. Attorney General the authority to inspect local and state voting records for federal elections.

The Second Consumer Revolution

In the 1950s, the country experienced stable inflation, employment rates, and economic growth. America experienced a second major consumer revolution as cars, televisions, and household appliances sold madly. The **National Highway Act** and the **GI Bill** stimulated suburban growth as young families left the cities for prefabricated starter homes. However, poor and minority families arrived in the wake of the "**white flight**" that had vacated downtown areas in cities such as Chicago and Detroit.

Beatniks and Nonconformists

Some people did not buy into the middle-class, suburban vision. Artists such as **Jackson Pollock** shocked the world with nonrepresentational paintings and characterized the modernist movement. Novelists such as **J. D. Salinger** challenged readers to think for themselves. *The Catcher in the Rye* shocked American parents as teens greedily read about the adventures of the troubled teen Holden Caulfield. Another group of nonconformists rocked New York's Greenwich Village with their poetry and wild culture. These "**beatniks**," such as **Jack Kerouac** and **Allen Ginsberg**, encouraged individuality in an age of conformity by using drugs freely.

Women and the Cult of Domesticity

Women of the 1950s were expected to take care of their "**baby boom**" offspring. Homemaking was exalted as the proper role for women, and women who left the home to work were scorned by their more traditional counterparts.

A Revolution in Science, Technology and Medicine

Electricity was now in 95 percent of homes. The electronics industry boomed in the 1950s as it raced to keep up with the demand for new and innovative products. Record players, refrigerators, and the "transistor radio" were revolutionary. Commercial airlines began to fly Americans around the world. **Penicillin**, discovered in the 1940s, now became widely available to doctors for treating bacterial infections. In 1955, in the wake of a deadly polio epidemic, **Dr. Jonas Salk** developed the **polio vaccine** that would almost eradicate the disease in United States by the 1960s.

❯❯ THE TURBULENT SIXTIES: 1960–1969

The John F. Kennedy (JFK) Presidency (Democrat), 1961–1963

As colonial governments in small Asian and African nations continued to fall, JFK changed Dulles's "new look" military to a "**flexible response**" military, which would root out communists in nations such as Vietnam and the Congo using conventional tactics and elite **special forces**. **The "New Frontier**," Kennedy's domestic agenda, succeeded in increasing the minimum wage and regulating steel prices.

THE CIVIL RIGHTS MOVEMENT IN THE KENNEDY YEARS

The "**Freedom Summer**" of 1961 was so named by the **Congress of Racial Equality (CORE),** which sent African Americans riding on integrated buses from the North towards the Deep South to test the Supreme Court–mandated desegregation of public transit. In Alabama, state police stood by watching while waiting mobs savagely beat the Freedom Riders. Attorney General Robert Kennedy sent in federal marshals to protect them, a victory for CORE. In 1962, JFK sent federal marshals to protect **James Meredith** as he became the first black student at the **University of Mississippi**. On Good Friday 1963, Dr. Martin Luther King Jr. marched on Birmingham, Alabama, after the city closed all its public facilities to avoid integration. King and his followers were arrested and jailed. During the two weeks in which he was locked up, Dr. King wrote his "**Letter from Birmingham Jail**," and the world watched in horror as the city's police commissioner **Eugene "Bull" Connor** used dogs, fire hoses, and cattle prods to disperse nonviolent protesters, of which many were children. In 1963, after Alabama governor **George Wallace** tried to keep African Americans from attending the University of Alabama, federal troops had to be summoned again. On August 28, 1963, Dr. King organized the **March on Washington**, D.C., the most successful march in U.S. history. His "**I Have a Dream**" speech touched audiences and lawmakers, and the **Civil Rights Act** passed soon after JFK was assassinated.

THE COLD WAR HEATS UP

The Bay of Pigs Invasion occurred in April of 1961, after Kennedy had approved Eisenhower's plans to invade Cuba. CIA operatives landed at Cuba's Bay of Pigs but were repelled by the locals.

THE BERLIN WALL

Soon after the Bay of Pigs fiasco, Kennedy met with Khrushchev in Vienna, and he refused to remove U.S. troops from Berlin. Khrushchev retaliated by building a wall around West Berlin, effectively stopping the flow of East Berliners to the West.

THE CUBAN MISSILE CRISIS

In October of 1962, U.S. spy planes discovered nuclear missile sites on Cuba. After Khrushchev and Castro refused to heed Kennedy's demand for immediate removal of the missiles, the United States began to blockade Soviet ships in the Atlantic Ocean. After several days of tension, Khrushchev agreed to remove the missiles from Cuba if the United States removed its missiles from Turkey and agreed never to invade Cuba again. Having come so close to nuclear war, the two leaders set up a hotline, "the **Red Phone**," through which they'd have immediate access to each other in times of crisis.

SOUTHEAST ASIAN AFFAIRS

When the French began pulling completely out of Vietnam, Kennedy increased financial and military assistance to the regimes in that country. The **Ngo Dinh Diem** regime was becoming more of a liability. Buddhist monks in **Saigon**, the South Vietnamese capital, set themselves on fire in protest of Ngo's discriminatory policies against Buddhists and the poor (who made up over 75 percent of the country's population), and a CIA-assisted assassination was carried out to remove Diem from power.

KENNEDY IS ASSASSINATED

On November 22, 1963, Kennedy's motorcade moved through the streets of Dallas, Texas. As America watched on television, the president was shot to death by **Lee Harvey Oswald**.

The Lyndon Baines Johnson (LBJ) Presidency (Democrat), 1963–1968

Vice President Johnson was sworn in as president aboard Air Force One. As his first act as president, he called for a special commission to investigate the assassination. That body, the **Warren Commission**, eventually concluded that Oswald had acted alone. After a year, LBJ ran for the presidency and continued on as an elected president. As JFK had done, Johnson wanted to expand civil rights, cut income taxes, and rid society of poverty. Influenced by **Michael Harrington**'s book, *The Other America*, which asserted that 20 percent of Americans and over 40 percent of African Americans lived in poverty, LBJ created the **Office of Equal Opportunity** (OEO) through which the **Job Corps**, which provided career training to inner-city and rural citizens, was formed. The OEO also ran the **Head Start Program**, which provided free or low-cost preschool to disadvantaged children. Carrying on FDR's New Deal legacy, the LBJ administration created **Medicare** and **Medicaid**, which provided low-cost medical care to the elderly and poor. The Department of **Housing and Urban Development** (HUD), founded in 1966, provided low-cost housing and federal funds aimed at ridding cities of urban blight. The **Immigration Act of 1965** admitted millions of Latin American and Asian immigrants to the United States. The **National Endowment for the Humanities**, which provided federal funding for artistic programs, and the **Department of Transportation** were also created.

THE CIVIL RIGHTS MOVEMENT IN THE JOHNSON ERA

The Twenty-Fourth Amendment, which abolished another barrier to voting rights by outlawing the poll tax, was ratified under LBJ. The **Civil Rights Act** of 1964 outlawed segregation in public places, and LBJ established the **Equal Employment Opportunity Commission** to enforce the law, making discrimination based on race, religion, ethnic origin, or gender illegal and the federal government responsible for finding and righting such bias. This enormous legislative success signaled the end of **de jure** (by law) segregation. However, to show that voting rights were still being denied, Dr. King organized a march from Selma to Montgomery, Alabama, in 1965. The march came to a violent end outside of Selma, as state police beat and taunted marchers. The **Voting Rights Act** of 1965 made literacy tests illegal and more or less nationalized the voter registration system in states where African Americans had been denied voting rights.

BLACK DISSENT

As some blacks grew tired of Dr. King's "love thy enemy" rhetoric, radical African American groups took issue with his teachings. Speaking for the **Nation of Islam** (**Black Muslims**), whose members followed the teachings of **Elijah Muhammad**, **Malcolm X** openly criticized Dr. King and his followers, calling them "**Uncle Toms**" who had sold out to whites. While not advocating the use of violence, Malcolm X did encourage self-defense as a violent response to violence. However, after Malcolm took his requisite Hajj (pilgrimage) to Mecca, he returned a changed man who now preached love and understanding. He left the Nation of Islam and was assassinated by members of the Nation as he spoke to a congregation in February 1965. Meanwhile, the once nonviolent SNCC changed course in 1966. Under the leadership of **Stokely Carmichael**, it rejected integration and began touting "**Black Power.**" Carmichael left SNCC for the Oakland, California-based **Black Panthers**, who openly carried weapons and clashed with police on a regular basis. Despite the violence, the Black Panthers organized the Oakland's black community, creating a self-sufficient network that provided free day care for working mothers and food for the poor, until the Panthers dissolved in the 1970s.

THE KERNER COMMISSION

After a series of race riots broke out in cities such as Los Angeles, Chicago, and Atlanta from 1964 to 1968, LBJ appointed the **Kerner Commission** to look into the problem. Its 1968 report concluded that frustration over extreme poverty and lack of opportunity had sparked the riots.

THE ASSASSINATION OF DR KING

On April 4, 1968, staying in Memphis in support of a sanitation workers' strike, Dr. King was assassinated as he looked out from his motel's balcony. In reaction, riots broke out across the country as African Americans expressed their anger with society.

LBJ AND VIETNAM

Vietnam was crumbling as LBJ took the oath of office, and Secretary of Defense **Robert McNamara** urged forceful action to prevent its fall. In August 1964, after a North Vietnamese gunboat attacked two U.S. destroyers in the Gulf of Tonkin, off North Vietnam's coast, the president asked Congress for authority to use military force without an actual war declaration. **The Gulf of Tonkin Resolution** greatly increased the power of the executive branch to engage in war. It was later discovered that the U.S. destroyers were actually assisting the South Vietnamese in attacking their northern neighbor and, thus, the attacks were not "unprovoked." Johnson used the Gulf of Tonkin Resolution to widen the war further after he won re-election in 1964. Backing out of Vietnam was not a good option, as the country would have certainly fallen into communist hands, while the cost of an escalated war would reduce funding available for LBJ's Great Society programs. In 1965, hoping for a quick end to the war, the president ordered bombing raids over North Vietnam (**Operation Rolling Thunder**). A quick victory was not in the cards, as **Ho Chi Minh**'s **Vietcong** and **Vietminh** still bounced back with more men and supplies. The United States focused on destroying the "**Ho Chi Minh Trail**," which linked the South Vietnamese Vietcong fighters with the North Vietnamese supply lines, and sent U.S. air and ground forces to fight in Vietnam's tropical jungle. The United States dropped more artillery on North Vietnam than in all of World War II. General William Westmoreland's "**search and destroy**" strategy involved rooting South Vietnam's Vietcong sympathizers out of villages by burning homes to the ground. In the United States, "**hawks**" (war supporters) and "**doves**" (opposed to the war) battled it out in Congress and public areas.

THE TET OFFENSIVE

In January of 1968, on **Tet**, the Vietnamese New Year, Vietcong forces surprised U.S. troops by attacking military bases as they launched a massive offensive that moved the war from the countryside to the streets of Saigon. It became clear that the communists had no intention of surrendering and would ultimately win. American public opinion now ran against the war, and the public demanded that the United States pull out of the war-torn country. LBJ lost half of his support in approval ratings and chose not to run for re-election in 1968.

The Counterculture

America's "baby boomers" became long-haired teenagers rebelling against the conformity of their parents' generation. These students were outspoken and willing to protest publicly about America's social, economic, and political wrongs. The "**New Left**" was born in 1962, when a group of college students led by **Tom Hayden** met in Port Huron, Michigan, to form the **Students for a Democratic Society** (**SDS**). The meeting yielded the **Port Huron Statement**, through which the students demanded a greater voice in the course of their lives. The **Free Speech Movement** (**FSM**) was formed in 1964 on the campus of the University of California–Berkeley. Berkeley students staged **sit-ins** protesting university policies and **teach-ins** about topics ranging from civil rights to the Vietnam War. Music united young people, who connected with folk singers such as **Bob Dylan** and **Joan Baez** and their songs of protest. A 1969 festival on a New York farm called **Woodstock** came to typify the youthful **counterculture**. **Hippies** gathered to hear musicians such as **Jimi Hendrix** and **Janis Joplin** and party. Though the three-day event became famous for sex, drugs, and rock and roll, Woodstock's **flower children** soon changed course to protest the Vietnam War.

Armed with the birth control pill and the ideas of the feminist movement, the counterculture also created the "**sexual revolution**" in the mid-60s, which softened Americans' views regarding sexual relationships and gender roles. After **Betty Friedan** founded the **National Organization for Women** (**NOW**) in 1966, the feminist movement gained more momentum and women began to demand a greater role in American society. Though the **Civil Rights Act of 1964** had made discrimination on the basis of gender illegal, women wanted something even stronger. The goal was almost realized in 1972, when Congress passed the **Equal Rights Amendment** (**ERA**) forbidding discrimination on the basis of sex, but the bill never got enough state votes to be ratified.

❯❯ THE THAWING OF THE COLD WAR: 1970–1990

The RFK Assassination

John F. Kennedy's younger brother, **Robert F. Kennedy** (**RFK**), ran for president and won the California primary. After giving a victory speech in Los Angeles's **Ambassador Hotel**, he was shot and killed by a young Palestinian nationalist named **Sirhan Sirhan.**

The Chicago Convention Riots

The Democratic Convention was held in Chicago. A large number of antiwar protesters converged on the city to protest Vice President **Hubert Humphrey**'s support of LBJ's war. Chicago's mayor, Richard C. Daley, sent in the police, who harassed and beat protesters. The resulting riot was broadcast to the nation and caused many to question both Daley and Humphrey. Humphrey did become the Democratic nominee, while Republicans gave **Richard M. Nixon** another try at the presidency. The **American Independent Party** rose to prominence when it chose Alabama segregationist Governor **George Wallace** as its candidate.

The Nixon Presidency (Republican), 1969–1974

Nixon narrowly won the presidency, but the Democrats maintained their majority in Congress. To garner more support from conservatives across the nation, he appealed to the so-called "**silent majority**"—conservative Democrats who were likely Southern, working-class, or elderly citizens who had become disenchanted by the liberalism of their party.

NIXON AND VIETNAM

With 500,000 Americans overseas in a very unpopular war, Nixon wanted a way to pull back slowly but still end the conflict with an "**honorable peace**." During the presidential campaign, he had referred to his "secret" plan to end the war, but he really had no idea how he was going to accomplish this. Nixon announced a plan to turn the war over to the Vietnamese. **Vietnamization** would occur as the U.S. military taught South Vietnam how to fight the war on its own. A gradual withdrawal began, and the number of U.S. troops in Vietnam decreased from over 500,000 in 1969 to just 30,000 in 1972. Nixon's efforts to end the war were questionable, as he escalated the war by secretly bombing Cambodia in 1970 to shut down the Ho Chi Minh Trail. When the U.S. media reported the bombing missions, the news spurred nationwide protest. National Guard troops sent to "keep the peace" shot and killed four students (who were passers-by, not protesters) at Ohio's **Kent State University** and two students at Mississippi's **Jackson State College**. In 1969, the nation was outraged after learning that U.S. troops had massacred Vietnamese women and children in the village of **My Lai** in 1968.

In 1971, government documents, known as the **Pentagon Papers**, that former Defense Department analyst Daniel Ellsberg had leaked to the *New York Times* revealed that a succession of administrations had lied to Congress. LBJ's real reason for continued involvement in Vietnam was to keep the United States from losing face, and the United States *had* provoked the Gulf of Tonkin incident. Meanwhile, Nixon's secretary of state, **Henry Kissinger**, was secretly negotiating with the North Vietnamese. Nixon knew South Vietnam would not be able to hold the communists off for very long on their own, so when the talks ground to a halt, he ordered some of the heaviest bombings yet to get North Vietnam back to the negotiating table. In 1973, the sides returned to the table in Paris to hammer out an agreement. The North Vietnamese would regain control of areas in the south, while the United States would pull out its troops in exchange for prisoners of war (POWs). The last U.S. troops pulled out on March 29, 1973. Saigon fell to the communists in April of 1975. In the end, the war killed or injured over 360,000 Americans, the Vietnamese lost over 2 million people, and the United States had spent $176 billion on the war. After learning of the secret bombings of Cambodia, Congress repealed the Gulf of Tonkin Resolution by enacting a **War Powers Act**, which would severely limit the president's ability to wage war without the consent of the legislative branch.

DÉTENTE WITH CHINA AND RUSSIA

President Nixon and Secretary of State Kissinger crafted **détente** (the relaxing of tensions) among the United States, the Soviet Union, and China. In February 1972, Nixon visited communist China to discuss policy with **Mao Tse-Tung**. Nixon reversed his previous stand when he agreed to support China's bid for admittance to the United Nations and officially recognized the Chinese Revolution. Nixon then visited Moscow to encourage the USSR to sign a nuclear arms limitation treaty. In the **Strategic Arms Limitation Treaty** (**SALT I**), signed by the United States and the USSR in May 1972, each nation agreed to reduce its number of nuclear missiles, and the United States promised to supply the Soviets with much-needed grain over the next three years, lessening the tension among the three world superpowers.

THE YOM KIPPUR WAR AND GAS SHORTAGES

In October 1973, on the Jewish holy day of **Yom Kippur**, war broke out between Israel and a Syria/Egypt coalition. After President Nixon sent Israel aid, which greatly boosted its forces and brought the war to a quick end, the

Organization of Petroleum Exporting Countries (OPEC) initiated an oil embargo to punish the United States for its involvement. The U.S. supply of gasoline and petroleum products fell, and the gas shortage ravaged the economy. Also, the new phenomenon of **"stagflation"** (high inflation coupled with high unemployment) made for an economy that was difficult to repair. After a disastrous attempt to curb inflation by cutting government spending, Nixon took the country off the gold standard to bring the value of U.S. currency down relative to foreign currencies. This stimulated foreign investment and spending in the United States and helped the economy recover.

WATERGATE AND ITS AFTERMATH

The Nixon presidency would be damaged beyond repair after the election of 1972. As *Washington Post* journalists Bob Woodward and Carl Bernstein investigated a pre-election (June 1972) break-in at the Democratic Party National Headquarters in Washington, D.C., they discovered that the burglars were connected to Nixon's **Committee to Reelect the President** (**CRP**, later nicknamed **CREEP**) and had been attempting to bug the headquarters. The Nixon White House had hoped to stop "**leaks**" by hiring "**plumbers**" who used wiretaps, coercion, and threats to keep people quiet. The Watergate break-in was just the tip of an iceberg of illegal activities linked to Nixon. A voice-activated tape system was discovered in the Oval Office. Congress demanded the tapes. Nixon refused, claiming that he was protected by executive privilege, and continued refusing for over a year. In the midst of all that, Vice President **Spiro Agnew** was convicted of tax evasion committed during his tenure as governor of Maryland and had to resign. The newly ratified **Twenty-Fifth Amendment,** which required the president to fill the vacant office, was enacted and Nixon chose Representative Gerald R. Ford as his new vice president. Facing certain impeachment and conviction by Congress (on the charges of obstruction of justice, abuse of power, and contempt), President Nixon resigned on August 9, 1974. The Oval Office recordings were only released after the Supreme Court (in *Nixon v. United States*, July 1974) ruled that Congress was entitled to examine them. The unedited tapes contained the "**smoking gun**" that directly linked the president to the Watergate scandal. Nixon's tenure is now known as an "**imperial presidency**," because the president claimed the right to keep documents from Congress and refused to spend funds appropriated by Congress by "impounding" them.

Gerald Ford Inherits the Presidency (Republican), 1974–1976

Vice President Gerald R. Ford became the only unelected president (not elected as either president or vice president) in history. He pardoned former president Nixon of all charges and tried to improve the economy through tax cuts and the reduction of government spending (to no avail). President Ford witnessed the failure of U.S. foreign policy in Asia, as Saigon and Cambodia both fell to the communists in 1975.

The Carter Presidency (Democrat), 1977–1980

A former Georgia governor, Jimmy Carter was a conservative Democrat from the South who appealed to Americans still reeling from Nixon's lies. He won the presidency with only 51 percent of the popular vote (which included 97 percent of the African American vote). Democrats also gained majorities in both houses of Congress. Carter granted **amnesty** to the 10,000 men who had fled the draft during the Vietnam War and created the **Department of Education** to address problems of weak public schools and the **Department of Energy** to deal with the energy crisis. The United States remained in an economic crisis until the mid-1980s.

THE CAMP DAVID ACCORDS

In 1978, President Carter invited Egypt's President **Anwar Sadat** and Israeli Prime Minister **Menachem Begin** to the presidential retreat at Camp David, Maryland, where he mediated a peace agreement that the two leaders signed in September 1978. The first step towards a Middle Eastern peace since Israel's founding in 1948, the Camp David Accords were Carter's greatest success.

THE IRAN HOSTAGE CRISIS

In 1979, Islamic fundamentalists overthrew America's ally, the Shah of Iran, and made the **Ayatollah Khomeini** ruler in his place. Now the United States had no real friend in the oil-rich region. When the Ayatollah cut off the flow of petroleum to OPEC, the United States had to live with another gasoline shortage. Iranian students who blamed the United States for supporting the shah when he ruled seized the American embassy in Tehran and took hostages. All the female and African American hostages were released within a few days, but 52 white men were held captive (and would remain so for the next 444 days). President Carter responded to the hostage taking by freezing Iranian assets in the United States. He also ordered a rescue mission, which failed and became a political liability.

THE SOVIET UNION, SALT II, AND AFGHANISTAN

Carter also had to deal with increasing tensions between the United States and the Soviet Union. SALT I (Strategic Arms Limitation Treaty) was set to expire in 1977, so Carter and the Soviets negotiated a renewal treaty. **SALT II** was ready for ratification when another world crisis got in the way. In December 1979, the USSR invaded **Afghanistan**. Certain that Soviets wanted a hold in the strategically important Persian Gulf, the United States stopped supplying the USSR with grain, withdrew SALT II from the table, and boycotted the 1980 **Moscow Olympic Games**.

The Reagan Presidency (Republican), 1981–1988

On Reagan's inauguration day, Iran suddenly released the hostages, starting his term on a high note. The "**Reagan Revolution**" ushered in a new era of conservative policy making in Washington. Reagan promised lower taxes, smaller government, and a stronger military. He believed in trickle-down economics and wanted to cut taxes and encourage the wealthy to spend. In 1981, Congress granted his tax cut, which would sum to 25 percent over a three-year period. As a result, many federally funded social programs were cut or killed altogether, while defense spending increased. Industries were **deregulated**, and other regulations, such as clean air standards for automobiles, were lifted to help struggling industries and large factories. Freed from regulation, the savings and loan industry began making risky investments to increase profits. By the mid-1980s, many of these institutions were in danger of collapsing. Later (in 1989), government failure to regulate the savings and loans would bear unpleasant fruit.

In August 1981, the nation's **air traffic controllers** decided to walk off the job illegally, and Reagan fired every one, replacing them with military personnel until civilians could be trained to take their place permanently. Thus, the air traffic controllers' union was destroyed.

SUPREME COURT APPOINTMENTS

Reagan wanted a reconfigured Supreme Court that would leave a more conservative legacy. He achieved this by seating **Sandra Day O'Connor**, the first woman on the Court, and placing conservatives **Antonin Scalia** and **Anthony Kennedy** on the bench as well. The new court pleased the conservative establishment by pulling back on laws protecting legal abortions, women, and African Americans.

THE *CHALLENGER* DISASTER

On February 1986, the NASA space shuttle *Challenger* exploded upon takeoff, killing all seven astronauts aboard.

THE IRAN-CONTRA SCANDAL

It was discovered that the Reagan administration was facilitating the supply of arms to the Nicaraguan "Contras" (something Congress had forbidden) and that a deal involving the sale of arms had been made with Iran in exchange for the release of the American hostages. When the scandal broke, the president denied any knowledge of those events.

BLACK MONDAY

On October 19, 1987, the nation witnessed the largest drop of the stock market since the Great Depression, after which Congress, fearing a return of recession, reduced taxes even further.

THE COLD WAR ENDS

President Reagan promised Americans a stronger military, called the Soviet Union the "**evil empire**," and pushed for the **Strategic Defense System** (**SDI**; "**Star Wars**"), an earth-orbiting defense system that would use lasers to defend the United States against nuclear attack. The "Star Wars" idea put intense pressure on the Soviets and was effective as a scare tactic. Then in 1985, **Mikhail Gorbachev**, a man with reformist ideas, came to power in the USSR. The first reform, **glasnost** (openness), was designed to rid the country of the old Stalin-era totalitarianism by easing the old laws that limited Russians' freedoms. **Perestroika** (restructuring) would open the Soviet economy to the free market. Gorbachev also decided to stop his country's arms buildup. In December 1987, Reagan and Gorbachev signed an agreement to rid the world of intermediate-range missiles.

The George H. W. Bush Presidency (Republican), 1989–1993

Bush, who had been Reagan's vice president, promised to be tough on crime and not to raise taxes. Though he was a Republican president, he had to work with a Democratic Congress since his party had not carried the House or the Senate.

THE LOS ANGELES RIOTS

In 1992, a Los Angeles jury acquitted white policemen in the beating of **Rodney King**, an African American man they had abused, and the city's minority communities erupted in violence. After three days of looting, arson, and murder, the city had sustained over $500 million in damage and lost 40 lives. The nation had witnessed the brutality of the initial incident—the videotape of Mr. King's arrest had been broadcast over and over.

FOREIGN EVENTS IN THE BUSH YEARS

In the spring of 1989, China's students demanded democracy. Beijing crushed this movement with ferocity, killing hundreds and jailing many more. In Europe, the Eastern Bloc countries were experiencing troubles and challenges, too, as Gorbachev told them that the Soviet Union could no longer provide them with military assistance. With the "**Solidarity**" movement, the rise of **Lech Walesa** in Poland, and the collapse of the Romanian government in 1989, the "iron curtain" was coming down in Europe. In October of 1989, German protestors tore down the Berlin Wall. The Soviet republics of Estonia, Latvia, and Lithuania declared their independence in the spring of 1990, and Gorbachev was forced from power as the Soviet Union collapsed on Christmas Day 1991. **Boris Yeltsin** became president of Russia, which joined with the 14 other former Soviet republics to form the temporary Commonwealth of Independent States. Presidents Bush and Yeltsin began to dismantle the nuclear war plans that had been built up over the past four decades and signed **START I** in 1991, which drastically reduced the number of nuclear warheads in both countries. **START II**, signed by both men in 1993, further reduced the number of warheads and promised Russia U.S. economic aid.

❯ POST–COLD WAR AMERICA

Demographic Shifts

Many changes altered the demographic makeup of the United States after the **Immigration Act of 1965** opened the doors to more foreigners. Between 1965 and 2000, Cubans, Indians, Koreans, Pakistanis, Chinese, Vietnamese, Filipinos, and Mexicans flocked to America. Texas, California, Arizona, and Florida experienced massive population growth. But most could not afford to provide education, medical care, and housing to documented residents and undocumented aliens. In 1986, Congress passed the **Immigration and Control Act**, aimed principally at the curtailing traffic of illegal immigrants across the U.S./Mexican border. By 1990, 12 million undocumented aliens had come into the country.

Increasing Mobility and Health

The **Interstate Highway Act** had provided easy-to-navigate freeways that connected every point across the United States, and Americans were on the move. Many left the former "**steel belt**" states (known as the "**Rust Belt**" after the steel factories had been forced out of business by decreasing domestic demand and increasing competition in the global marketplace) and moved to the **Sun Belt**. Aerospace jobs lured the nation's best and brightest to California, Texas, Arizona, Florida, and New Mexico, where they could even stay cool thanks to (recently invented) air-conditioning.

The stuff of science fiction became reality as technology advanced from the 1965 to 2000. Advances in biotechnology, mass communications, and computers made the world a much smaller place, bringing excitement, progress, and new dangers to society. Through such medical advances as organ transplants, artificial life support, and advanced drug therapies, human life can be saved and extended through modern science. Once-deadly bacterial diseases can now be treated with a single regimen of antibiotics. In 2003, U.S. researchers successfully mapped the entire **human genome**, and **stem cell** research is underway. Despite these advances, the **Acquired Immune Deficiency Syndrome (AIDS)** virus descended upon urban areas in the 1980s and soon spread worldwide.

The Internet

In mid-century, computers were room-sized mainframes. Much smaller, more powerful computers became possible with the invention of transistors and microprocessors. Wanting to get into the new **personal computer** market, IBM introduced the IBM PC in 1981. The PC used parts from other manufacturers and a third-party operating system (MS-DOS). It had an open architecture, allowing other companies to create add-ons. All of this made it easy to duplicate, and the market soon filled with PCs from other vendors. With a few exceptions—notably the Apple Macintosh—personal computers that weren't IBM compatible died out. By the mid-1990s, laptops could outperform their mainframe predecessors by a huge margin.

In 1969, **ARPANET** linked computers at four universities. It steadily grew, used mostly by research institutions and government agencies. By the 1990s, it had evolved into the **Internet**, and it became available to the wider public. It would become ubiquitous by the 21st century, displacing other networks such as CompuServe and America Online.

Environmental Problems

As world population grows at an alarming rate, issues concerning biodiversity, genetically engineered foods, global warming, and natural disasters will continue to trouble human beings. The United States has experienced its fair share of environmental problems since 1965. President Carter addressed these when he created the Department of Energy and established **superfund sites** (former chemical waste dumps to be acquired and cleaned up for future use). Carter also encouraged the use of renewable energy sources such as solar power and started the Drive 55 plan to reduce gasoline use. In 1979, when a cloud of radioactive gas was released into the air from Pennsylvania's **Three Mile Island** nuclear plant, Americans learned that dangerous shortcuts had been taken in a rush to get the plant in operation. Many environmental measures were reversed by Presidents Reagan and George H. W. Bush in the interests of business.

The William Clinton Presidency (Democrat), 1993–2001

President Clinton worked to reform health care and the welfare system. The Republican Congress, led by House Speaker **Newt Gingrich**, twice pushed the president to a budget showdown, as Clinton vetoed the Republican budget and forced all government offices to close until a new budget could be drawn up.

NORTH AMERICAN FREE TRADE AGREEMENT (NAFTA)

In his first term, President Clinton dealt with globalization as it pertained to protecting American jobs and welfare. **NAFTA** opened free trade with Canada and Mexico, allowing more goods, services, and jobs to flow across their borders. Organized labor and conservative groups opposed NAFTA, feeling that it sold out American jobs for cheap, foreign labor and compromised America's sovereignty to international arbitration boards. Signed in 1993, NAFTA reduced restrictions and tariffs on goods and services transported between the United States, Canada, and Mexico.

THE OKLAHOMA CITY BOMBING

In 1995, the **Murrow Federal Building** in Oklahoma City, Oklahoma, was attacked by a large bomb that killed 168 people after right-wing extremist **Timothy McVeigh** and a set of accomplices drove a truck loaded with explosives near the building and triggered it by remote.

FOREIGN TERRORISTS

Fundamentalist Islamist groups were forming in countries such as Saudi Arabia, Iran, Syria, and Afghanistan. While some were established solely for protest purposes, others created a worldwide paramilitary network to fight the American "infidels." **Al-Qaeda**, led by Saudi national **Osama Bin Laden**, had a military training camp in Afghanistan that prepared warriors to attack Western targets. Using American funding and training from the 1980s, Bin Laden had successfully trained a multinational force of fighters and terrorists by the early 1990s. In 1993, Al-Qaeda attacked the World Trade Center in New York in 1993, killing six people but inflicting minimal damage.

The George W. Bush Presidency (Republican), 2001–2009

On **September 11, 2001**, America was attacked by 19 terrorists affiliated with **Al-Qaeda**. In a coordinated suicide mission, a passenger jet crashed into the north tower of New York City's **World Trade Center**. Another plane crashed into the south tower about 15 minutes later, and yet another jet crashed into the Pentagon, and another went down in Pennsylvania. The twin towers collapsed, and everyone still inside, including the rescue workers who had rushed in to help, was killed. Some 3,000 lives were lost, the city of New York faced over $80 billion in damages, and the impact on U.S. business was devastating. The Bush administration immediately enacted the **USA PATRIOT Act** as part of **"the War on Terror,"** which broadly expanded the government's ability to monitor the activities of Americans and conduct investigations of suspected terrorists. Congress dispatched troops to Afghanistan, the home of Al-Qaeda and **Osama Bin Laden**, immediately after the attacks. In October 2001, U.S. troops invaded Afghanistan, whose ruling **Taliban** had given Al-Qaeda a safe haven. Though the U.S. military overthrew the Taliban and installed a coalition government in its place, Bin Laden repeatedly eluded capture. In post-9/11 America, hundreds of illegal and legal immigrants were arrested or assumed to be terrorists. President Bush insisted on invading **Iraq** in March 2003 in an effort to remove a potentially threatening dictator and his alleged cache of "weapons of mass destruction." Iraq had been a thorn in the side of the Bush family since the first President Bush's attempt to liberate Kuwait in 1991. Saddam Hussein was still in power and refusing to cooperate with United Nations weapons inspections. Bush and British Prime Minister Tony Blair convinced Congress that Iraq would be a serious threat to the world if left in power. The official invasion of Iraq was not sanctioned by the United Nations and was condemned by many U.S. allies around the world.

THINGS TO REMEMBER

PEOPLE

Mao Tse-Tung
Dwight D. Eisenhower
Fidel Castro
Alger Hiss
Joseph McCarthy
Department of Defense
National Security Council
Central Intelligence
  Agency (CIA)
South East Asian Treaty
  Organization (SEATO)

Nationalists (Koumintang)
House Un-American
  Activities Committee
  (HUAC)
National Aeronautics and
  Space Administration
  (NASA)
Dr. Martin Luther King Jr.
Rosa Parks
Jonas Salk
Warren Court

Little Rock Nine
Student Nonviolent
  Coordinating Committee
Richard M. Nixon
John F. Kennedy
Malcolm X
Stokely Carmichael
Ho Chi Minh
Sirhan Sirhan
Henry Kissinger
Anwar Sadat

Menachem Begin
Ayatollah Khomeini
George H. W. Bush
William (Bill) Clinton
Timothy McVeigh
Osama Bin Laden
George W. Bush
Saddam Hussein
Hillary Clinton
Barack Obama

EVENTS

Geneva Convention
Cuban Missile Crisis
New Frontier
Freedom Summer

Woodstock
Tet Offensive
Yom Kippur War
Reagan Revolution

Iran-Contra Scandal
Solidarity movement
"War on Terror"
9/11

Watts Riots
Hurricane Katrina

TERMS

Berlin Airlift
brinksmanship
massive retaliation
S.O.S.
red phone
McCarthyism
Sputnik
white flight
beatniks
Warren Commission
Office of Equal
  Opportunity

The Department of
  Housing and Urban
  Development
Nation of Islam
Kerner Commission
Vietcong
National Organization
  of Women
American Independent
  Party
Organization of Petroleum
  Exporting Countries

Committee to Re-elect
  the President
Commonwealth of
  Independent States
Vietnamization
détente
stagflation
Challenger
Star Wars
glasnost
perestroika
executive privilege

superfund site
AIDS
weapons of mass
  destruction
World Wide Web
Internet
reverse discrimination
Al-Qaeda
Taliban

PLACES

Aswan Dam
Bay of Pigs

Ho Chi Minh Trail

Berlin Wall

Three Mile Island

DOCUMENTS AND LAWS

Truman Doctrine
Marshall Plan
Warsaw Pack
National Security Act
Eisenhower Doctrine
Smith Act
Brown v. Board of
  Education

National Highway Act
The Feminine Mystique
Great Society
Immigration Act of 1965
Civil Rights Act of 1964
Voting Rights Act of 1965
Gulf of Tonkin Resolution
Port Huron Statement

Equal Rights Amendment
War Powers Act
Strategic Arms Limitation
  Treaty (SALT I)
Camp David Accords
SALT II
START I
Immigration Act of 1965

Immigration and Control
  Act of 1986
Proposition 209
International Monetary
  Fund (IMF)
North American Free Trade
  Agreement (NAFTA)
USA PATRIOT Act

Practice Section

❯ FREE-RESPONSE QUESTION

The following is a sample free-response question that you might see on the AP U.S. History exam. Listed under the question are important terms that would greatly add to your answer. AP Readers will look for you to mention at least several of the listed people, places, and things.

Suggested time: 35 minutes

What significant social, political, and economic challenges will the United States face through the next half century?

Study List:

the "graying" of America	minority-majority	homeland security
Social Security	equal pay for equal work	nuclear threats from rogue nations
health care	gay rights	global debt
welfare	religious rights	environmental protection
immigration	global terrorism	depletion of fossil fuels

❯ SCORING GUIDE

Monitoring your own success on the exam's essay section is straightforward. The scoring guides for the DBQ and the FRQ are very similar. Essays on the AP U.S. History exam are all scored on a nine-point scale. Basic requirements hold true from year to year, with the content requirements changing for each question asked. A standard nine-point scoring guide would look something like this:

The 8–9 essay

- Contains a clear, well-developed thesis that answers all parts of the prompt.
- Thesis is supported with substantial, relevant information.
- Provides evidence of thoughtful analysis.
- May contain minor errors.

The 5–7 essay

- Contains a thesis that answers all parts of the prompt; may be unbalanced.
- Thesis is supported with some relevant information.
- Analysis is unbalanced and/or limited.
- May contain errors that do not seriously detract from the quality of the essay.

The 2–4 essay

- Contains a confused or unfocused thesis or may simply restate the question.
- Contains minimal or irrelevant information or simply lists facts with no explanation.
- Contains little or no evidence of analysis and only a general treatment of information.
- May contain substantial errors.

The 0–1 essay

- Lacks a thesis or rewrites the question.
- Incompetent or inappropriate response.
- Shows little or no understanding of the question.
- Contains major factual errors.

The "–" essay

- Is blank or off-topic.

Essays are scored holistically, with Faculty Consultants (Exam Readers) reviewing each essay from beginning to end. Only actual essays are scored, which means that even if you have a great outline of an essay, you will receive a score of "–" if you do not write the essay in full.

❯ SAMPLE STUDENT RESPONSE

The most important political, social, and economic challenges that the United States will face in the coming half century will all stem from one key issue—oil. As the population of the world swells, global demand for oil will grow as well. If global production cannot keep up with global demand, then the entire world will be faced with massive shortages, price increases, and the possibility of another world war. The United States, the largest consumer of oil in the world, will be hardest hit by any fluctuations in the supply of oil.

Current global production of refined oil is not meeting demand. Americans see proof of this at gas stations across the country. The rise in cost is not due to a dwindling oil supply. Instead it is caused in part by the emerging need for refined oil in China, which is stressing global refining capacity. High prices now show what happens when the global market cannot keep up with global demand. Though oil industry experts cannot agree on when the world's oil reserves will be exhausted, they all agree on one thing—that it will happen. As the oil supply dwindles, it will no longer be enough for the huge U.S. economy. At first prices will rise, like what is happening now. But prices will not level off after a temporary adjustment period, as they are predicted to after the current price increase. They will keep rising, first handicapping the mass population, then small businesses, and finally large businesses.

Our economy, which has come to rely on cheap and abundant fuel, will suddenly have neither. This is what happened during the gas crisis of 1973, only world oil production was intentionally cut by OPEC. The result of the gas crisis was a year-long recession for the United States and the rest of the world. If a relative hiccup in oil production did that much damage to the U.S. economy back then, what will happen to the future economy when production can no longer support the demand?

The lack of oil will change the political sphere of the United States as well. Because oil is of paramount importance to the economy, it has the potential to become a significant issue in political campaigns. As the supply decreases, differing opinions will emerge on what to do about the coming crisis. Politicians will align themselves with philosophies that range from extreme conservation to threatening war on oil-rich countries. Already, U.S. foreign policy is geared toward placating powerful oil-producing countries and subjugating less powerful ones. Just look at U.S. relations with Saudi Arabia, a country with a dubious, but conveniently overlooked, human rights record, and Iraq, a country that has been literally re-created by a U.S. occupation following a preemptive war with an equally dubious justification.

Oil will also affect American society. Oil is used for a lot more things than gasoline. Oil is a key ingredient in such widely used materials as plastics, pesticides, fertilizers, lubricants, and many other chemicals. If the supply of oil were to evaporate, not only would the American consumer not be able to fill up the gas tank of his car, he would have a car with a significantly smaller amount of plastic (a larger component of a modern car than is obvious to the naked eye), and his car would need to run on synthetic lubricant. Alternatives to petroleum products already exist, but the demand for such products will increase exponentially once oil becomes a rarity. Americans will have to rethink their daily lives. They will need to use more public transportation in a country that has been developed around the family car since the era of Henry Ford. People who live in colder areas will need to find a way to heat their homes without oil or gas. And because there doesn't seem to be a quick and easy replacement for oil in a world that depends on it, the cost of available energy from other sources will be far beyond the average consumer's reach, creating a whole new societal class, the non-mobile, educated workforce.

Though the loss of oil is only one challenge that the United States will face in the coming 50 years, it is the linchpin of our society, and its absence will have devastating effects on our way of life politically, culturally, and especially economically.

U.S. History Glossary

abolitionist one who favors the end of slavery

affirmative action policies of the government aimed at increasing access to jobs, schooling, and opportunities to people previously discriminated against

agrarian pertaining to farming or agriculture

anarchist an individual who advocates the overthrow of all government

annexation the act of adding a smaller territory to a larger one

antebellum before the war; usually used with regard to the time before the Civil War

anti-Semitic having or showing prejudice against Jews

apologists those in the South who justified slavery by claiming African Americans were better off under the current system than left on their own

appeasement a policy of giving into modest demands of an enemy to hold off potential conflict

apportionment the proportional distribution of the number of members of the U.S. House of Representatives on the basis of the population of each state

arbitration the settlement of a dispute by a third, unbiased party

armistice a suspension of fighting; a cease-fire

autocrat a ruler having unlimited power; a despot

bandwagon a political cause that draws increasing numbers of proponents due to its success

bicameral composed of or based on two legislative chambers or branches

blasphemy a contemptuous or profane act or writing concerning God or a sacred entity

blitzkrieg Hitler's tactic of "lightning war," which involved swift action against the enemy

bond an interest-bearing note issued by a government that promises repayment on a set date

boycott to refrain from purchasing or trading with another as an expression of protest

bracero a Mexican farm worker brought to the United States to work during World War II

buying on margin the act of purchasing stock on credit

capitalism an economic system in which the means of production and exchange are controlled by individuals

caravel any of several types of small, light sailing ships, especially one with two or three masts and lateen sails used by the Spanish and Portuguese in the 15th and 16th centuries

carpetbagger a Northern Republican who moved South for financial and political gain

ceded given or surrendered to another, possibly by treaty

charter a written grant from the sovereign power of a country conferring certain rights and privileges on a person, a corporation, or the people

closed shop a workplace in which workers must join the labor union as a result of employment

collective bargaining the process by which employees and management negotiate wages, working conditions, and work hours

confederation an alliance or body of states loosely united for common purposes

conscription compulsory enrollment of men in the armed forces

constituents the citizens of a particular region represented by an elected official

conquistador a Spanish conqueror of the Americas

conversion experience a rite of passage for Calvinists who publicly confessed all sins to become one of the "elect"

corollary an inference that follows proof from a previous instance

coup the overthrow of a ruling party/person by a small group illegally and/or by force

de facto "in fact"; usually with regard to segregation

de jure "in law"; usually with regard to laws passed for segregation

demography the study of the characteristics of human populations, such as size, growth, density, distribution, and vital statistics

depression a prolonged period of declining economic activity characterized by rising unemployment and falling prices

détente a period of relaxed tensions between countries

direct primary an election in which registered members of the party elect their party nominees

domestic of or relating to a country's internal affairs

duty money collected by government from a tariff

foreclosure the repossession of a property by a lender after a borrower fails to pay the loan

egalitarian upholding the equality of all people

elect according to Calvinists, those who have been chosen by God for salvation

elite a group or class of persons or a member of such a group or class enjoying superior intellectual, social, or economic status

emancipation to free from slavery or bondage

embargo a prohibition or ban; usually used with regard to trade or shipping

encomienda the Spanish labor system whereby individuals were bound to unpaid labor but were not legally owned by a master

enfranchisement giving the right to vote

entrepreneur a person who engages in a risky business adventure

established church a church that is officially recognized and protected by the government

excise tax a fee collected on goods and services bought and sold within a country

executive privilege the claim by a president that certain information should be kept from Congress

expatriates individuals who have chosen to leave their native country in favor of living abroad

fascism a dictatorial form of government that glorifies military service and nationalism

filibuster the act of members of Congress to delay a vote or action by refusing to release the floor during debate

fundamentalism a religious movement or point of view characterized by a return to rigid adherence to fundamental principles

gentry people of gentle birth, good breeding, or high social position; usually landowners

ghetto an area where ethnic minorities are forced to live, either by law or discrimination

graft the use of one's position to gain money or property illegally

greenback paper currency in the United States that replaced specie before the founding of the Federal Reserve

gross national product (GNP) the sum of all goods and services produced both within and abroad by citizens of a country in a given year

headright system a system of obtaining land in colonial times in which one received 50 acres of land for every emigrant to America one sponsored

horizontal integration complete control of one aspect of the manufacture of a product by a single company

impeach to charge a government official with a criminal offense

imperialism a policy of extending a country's authority over a foreign country by colonization

incumbent an individual running for an office he or she currently holds

indentured servant a person who is bonded or contracted to work for another for a specified time in exchange for learning a trade or for travel expenses

inflation an increase in the volume of money resulting in a decrease in the value of currency (i.e., rising prices)

infrastructure the basic structure needed for the functions of a society; usually transportation, sanitation, and communication

initiative process by which voters can propose legislation and place that law on a ballot in a popular election

insurrection the act of open revolt against civil authority or a constituted government

isolationist an individual who would rather the country remain uninvolved in world affairs

Jim Crow the practice of legal racial segregation

jingoism extreme nationalism coupled with an aggressive foreign policy stance

joint-stock company a company that has some features of a corporation and some features of a partnership

laissez-faire the belief that government should refrain from interfering in business and the economy

lynching the illegal act of hanging to death a person accused of committing a crime

mandate a command or instruction given by the electorate to their representative

martial law military occupation imposed upon an area when civilian resources have failed

mercantilism the belief that all economic activity should be for the good of the whole (country) rather than for the individual

mercenaries foreign soldiers hired to serve in the military

mestizo a person of mixed racial ancestry, especially of mixed European and Native American ancestry

mudslinging unsubstantiated accusations and attacks on a political opponent

mulatto an individual of African and European ancestry

nation-state a political society that combines a central government with cultural unification

nativism the policy of upholding the rights of native citizens over those of immigrants

naturalization the process of immigrants gaining citizenship

nullify to declare a law void

omnibus bill a potential law that includes a variety of topics under one name

partisan supporting a particular political party

political machine an organization controlled through spoils and patronage

poll tax a tax levied on individuals before they can vote

pool an alliance of competing companies to set prices and split profits by sharing customers

pork barrel congressional appropriations for political gain in a particular constituency

precedent a decision or action that establishes a standard for future instances

predestination the doctrine that God has foreordained all things, especially that God has elected certain souls to eternal salvation

propaganda information or materials provided by the proponents or opponents of an idea to influence public thought

proprietary colony a settlement in a region granted by a king or queen to a legal owner

proviso a clause within a document that stipulates an exception or restriction

pump priming an increase in government spending to stimulate the economy

quota a proportional share of something to a group or members of a group; an allotment

ratification the act of approving and giving formal sanction to

recall the act of removing a public official from office by a vote of a specified number of citizens

referendum the submission of a law directly to the voters for approval or denial

reparations money, goods, or services paid by a government for damage caused during a war

secession the withdrawal from an alliance or association

sedition the act of incitement of rebellion against the government

sharecropper an individual who receives land on credit and pays back debt with a share of the crop yield

socialist an individual who believes that business and the economy should be controlled by the community, not individuals

specie coined (gold, silver, or other metal) currency

speculation risky business transactions on the bet of quick or considerable profit

spoils system the practice of the winning political party rewarding supporters with jobs, regardless of their qualifications

stagflation a combination of high unemployment and high inflation

strike an action by organized labor to stop work in order to force management to negotiate

suffrage the right to vote

tariffs taxes placed on imported goods

temperance the belief in moderation, particularly with regard to alcohol

theocracy a government by the church leaders

trust an organization of corporations where stockholders have traded their stocks for trust certificates

utopian seeking perfection in society

vertical integration control of all aspects of manufacturing by a single company

virtual representation the political practice of a small group of people being elected to speak for a larger group

wildcat banks uncontrolled and unregulated western banks of the 1800s whose speculation and unsafe practices helped spur the Panic of 1819

writ of habeas corpus from the Latin "of the body," a formal order requiring the presentation of the accused before a judge to be charged with a crime or released from custody

yellow-dog contracts agreements that forced employees to promise never to join a union in order to gain or maintain employment

yeomen non-slave-owning farmers

Index